KYLE BAKER

NAT TURNER™

Volume Two: Revolution

IMAGE COMICS, INC.

BERKELEY, CA.

NAT TURNER VOL. 2 OF 2: REVOLUTION

NAT TURNER, VOL. 2 (OF 2): REVOLUTION. 2007. PUBLISHED BY IMAGE COMICS, INC., OFFICE OF PUBLICATION: 1942 UNIVERSITY AVENUE, SUITE 305, BERKELEY, CALIFORNIA 94704. COPYRIGHT © 2007 KYLE BAKER. ALL RIGHTS RESERVED. NAT TURNER™ (INCLUDING ALL PROMINENT CHARACTERS FEATURED HEREIN), ITS LOGO AND ALL CHARACTER LIKENESSES ARE TRADEMARKS OF KYLE BAKER, UNLESS OTHERWISE NOTED. IMAGE COMICS® IS A TRADEMARK OF IMAGE COMICS, INC. ALL RIGHTS RESERVED. NO PART OF THIS PUBLICATION MAY BE REPRODUCED OR TRANSMITTED, IN ANY FORM OR BY ANY MEANS (EXCEPT FOR SHORT EXCERPTS FOR REVIEW PURPOSES) WITHOUT THE EXPRESS WRITTEN PERMISSION OF IMAGE COMICS, INC. ALL NAMES, CHARACTERS, EVENTS AND LOCALES IN THIS PUBLICATION ARE ENTIRELY FICTIONAL. ANY RESEMBLANCE TO ACTUAL PERSONS (LIVING OR DEAD), EVENTS OR PLACES, WITHOUT SATIRIC INTENT, IS COINCIDENTAL.

Published by

IMAGE COMICS

1942 UNIVERSITY AVE., SUITE 305, BERKELEY, CA 94704

VISIT WWW.KYLEBAKER.COM

ISBN-10: 1-58240-792-2

ISBN 13: 978-1-58240-792-0

FIRST PRINTING 2007

10 9 8 7 6 5 4 3 2 1

Printed in Canada

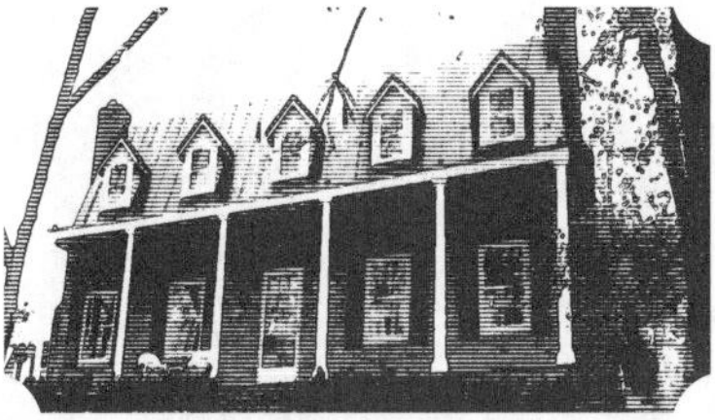

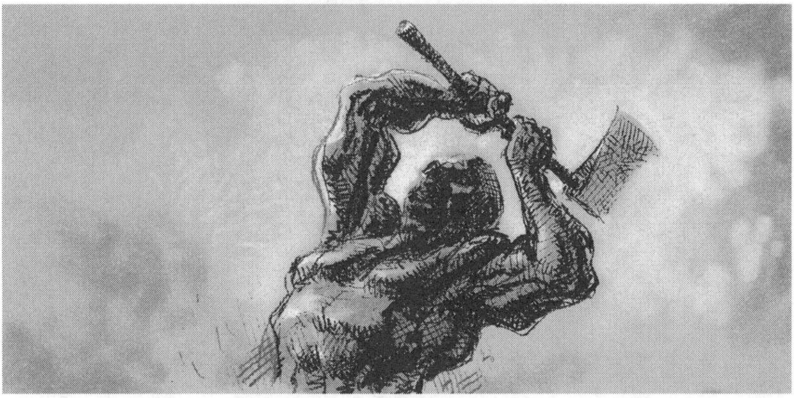

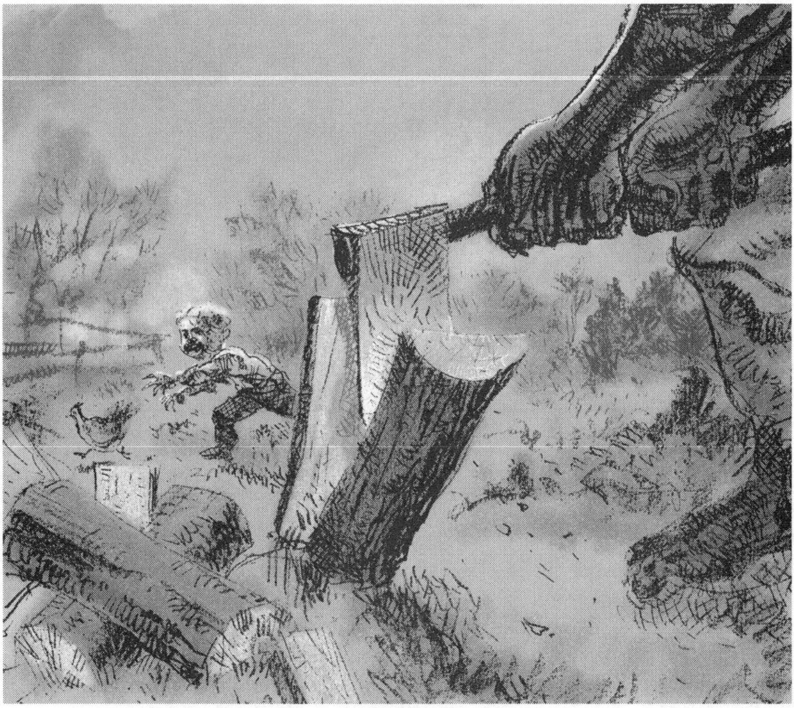

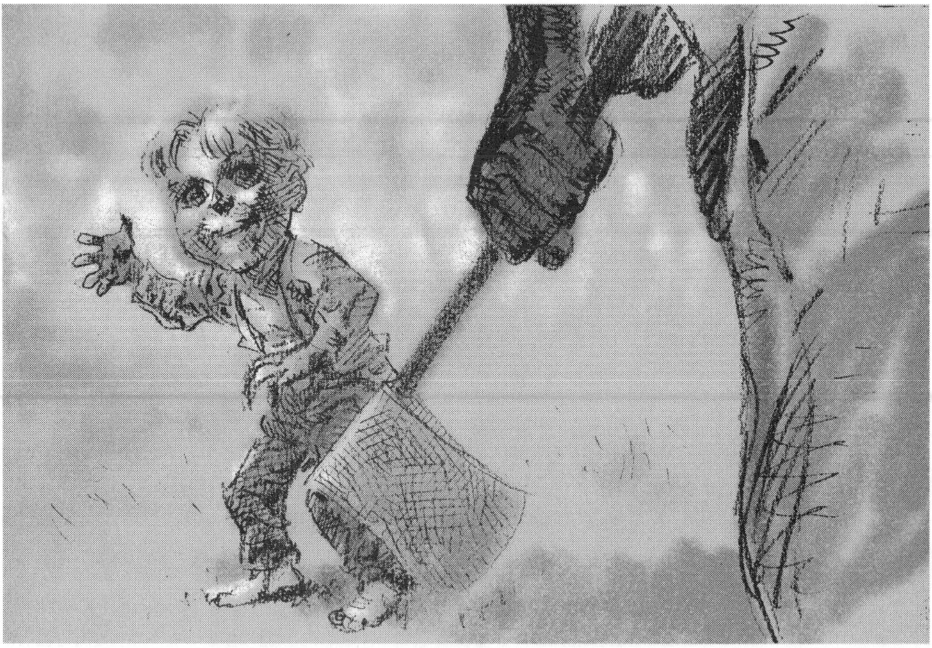

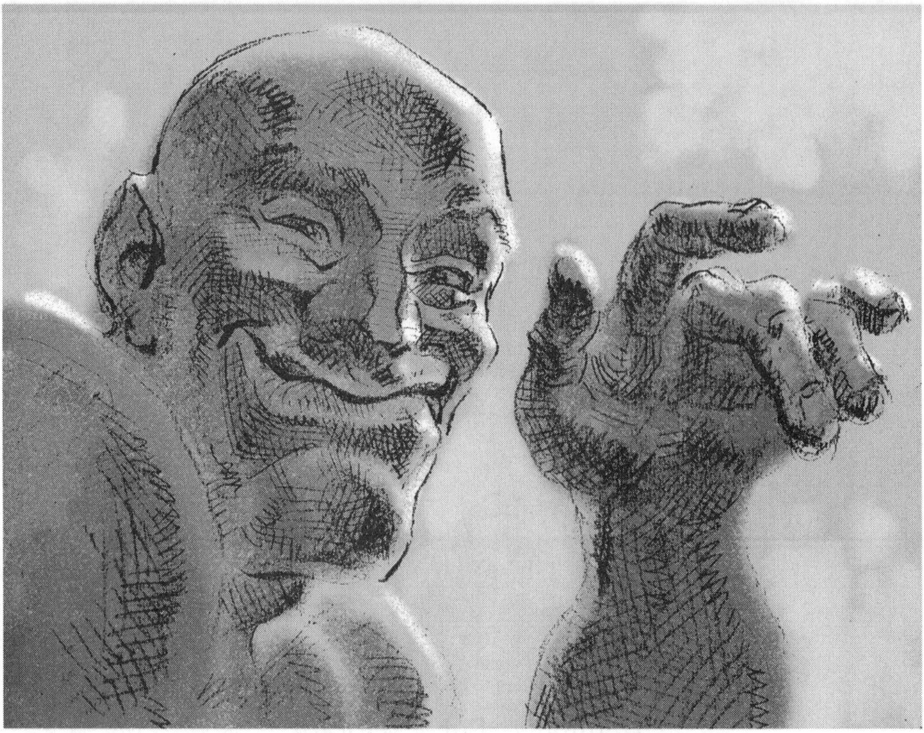

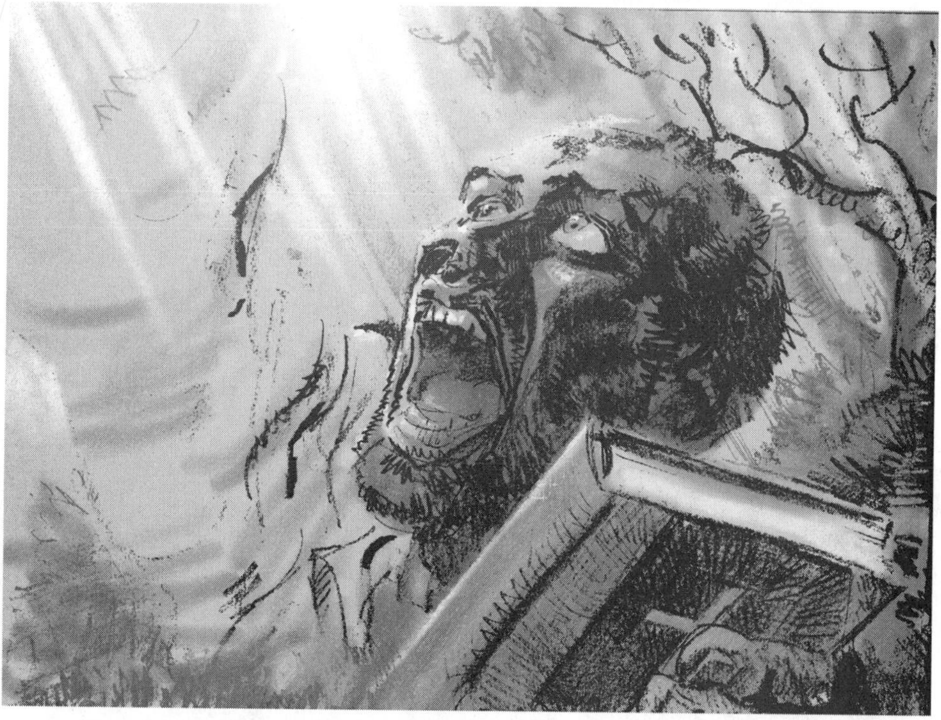

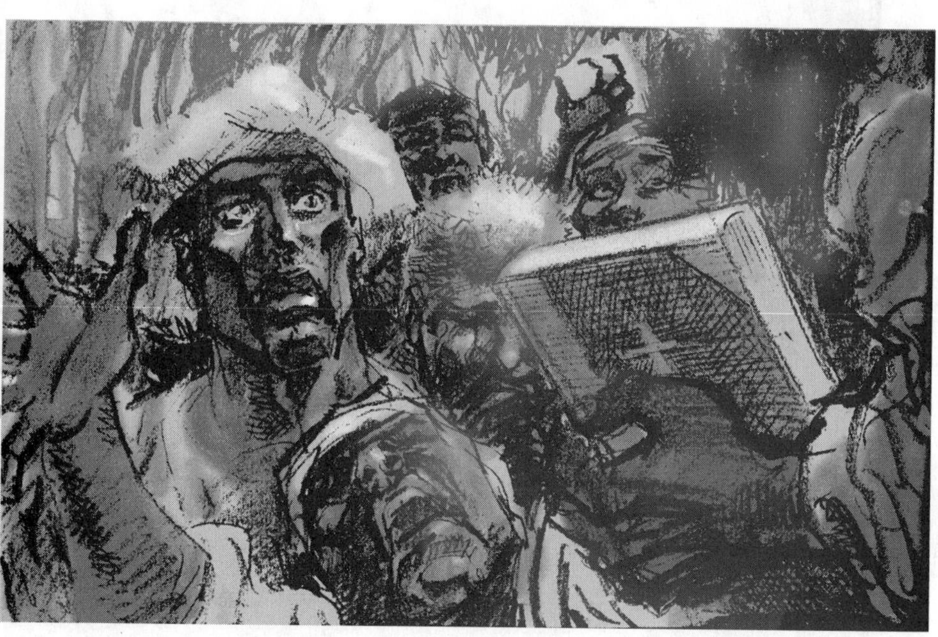

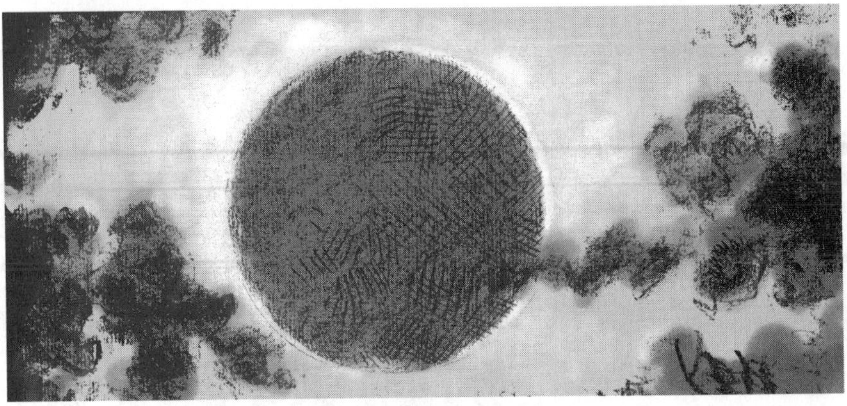

FROM THE CONFESSION OF NAT TURNER

"And by signs in the heavens that it would make known to me when I should commence the great work - and until the first sign appeared, I should conceal it from the knowledge of men - And on the appearance of the sign, (the eclipse of the sun last February) I should arise and prepare myself, and slay my enemies with their own weapons.

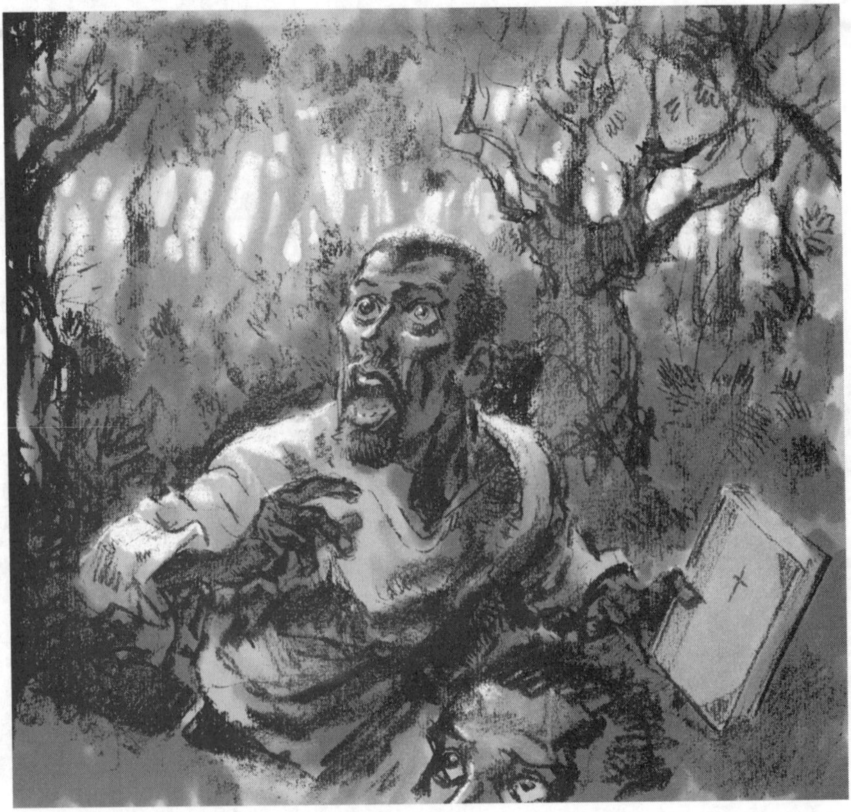

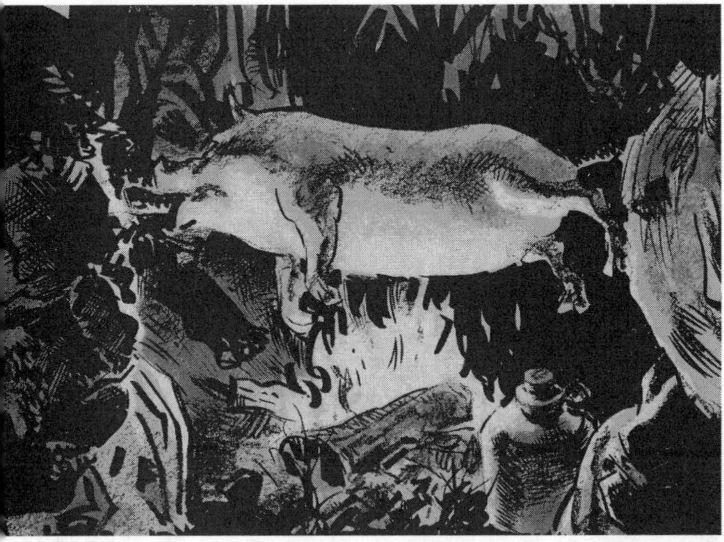

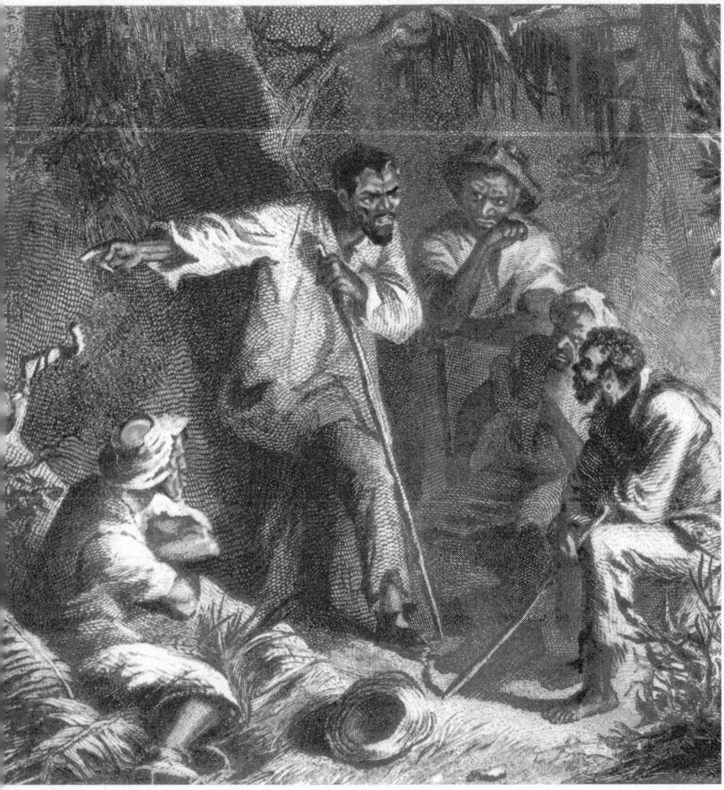

"And immediately on the sign appearing in the heavens, the seal was removed from my lips, and I communicated the great work laid out for me to do, to four in whom I had the greatest confidence - It was intended by us to have begun the work of death on the 4th of July last - Many were the plans formed and rejected by us, and it affected my mind to such a degree, that I fell sick, and the time passed without our coming to any determination how to commence - Still forming new schemes and rejecting them, when the sign appeared again, which determined me not to wait longer.

"IT WAS QUICKLY AGREED WE SHOULD COMMENCE AT HOME (MR. J. TRAVIS') ON THAT NIGHT, AND UNTIL WE HAD ARMED AND EQUIPPED OURSELVES, AND GATHERED SUFFICIENT FORCE, NEITHER AGE NOR SEX WAS TO BE SPARED, (WHICH WAS INVARIABLY ADHERED TO.) WE REMAINED AT THE FEAST UNTIL ABOUT TWO HOURS IN THE NIGHT, WHEN WE WENT TO THE HOUSE AND FOUND AUSTIN; THEY ALL WENT TO THE CIDER PRESS AND DRANK, EXCEPT MYSELF. ON RETURNING TO THE HOUSE, HARK WENT TO THE DOOR WITH AN AXE, FOR THE PURPOSE OF BREAKING IT OPEN, AS WE KNEW WE WERE STRONG ENOUGH TO MURDER THE FAMILY, IF THEY WERE AWAKED BY THE NOISE; BUT REFLECTING THAT IT MIGHT CREATE AN ALARM IN THE NEIGHBORHOOD, WE DETERMINED TO ENTER THE HOUSE SECRETLY, AND MURDER THEM WHILST SLEEPING.

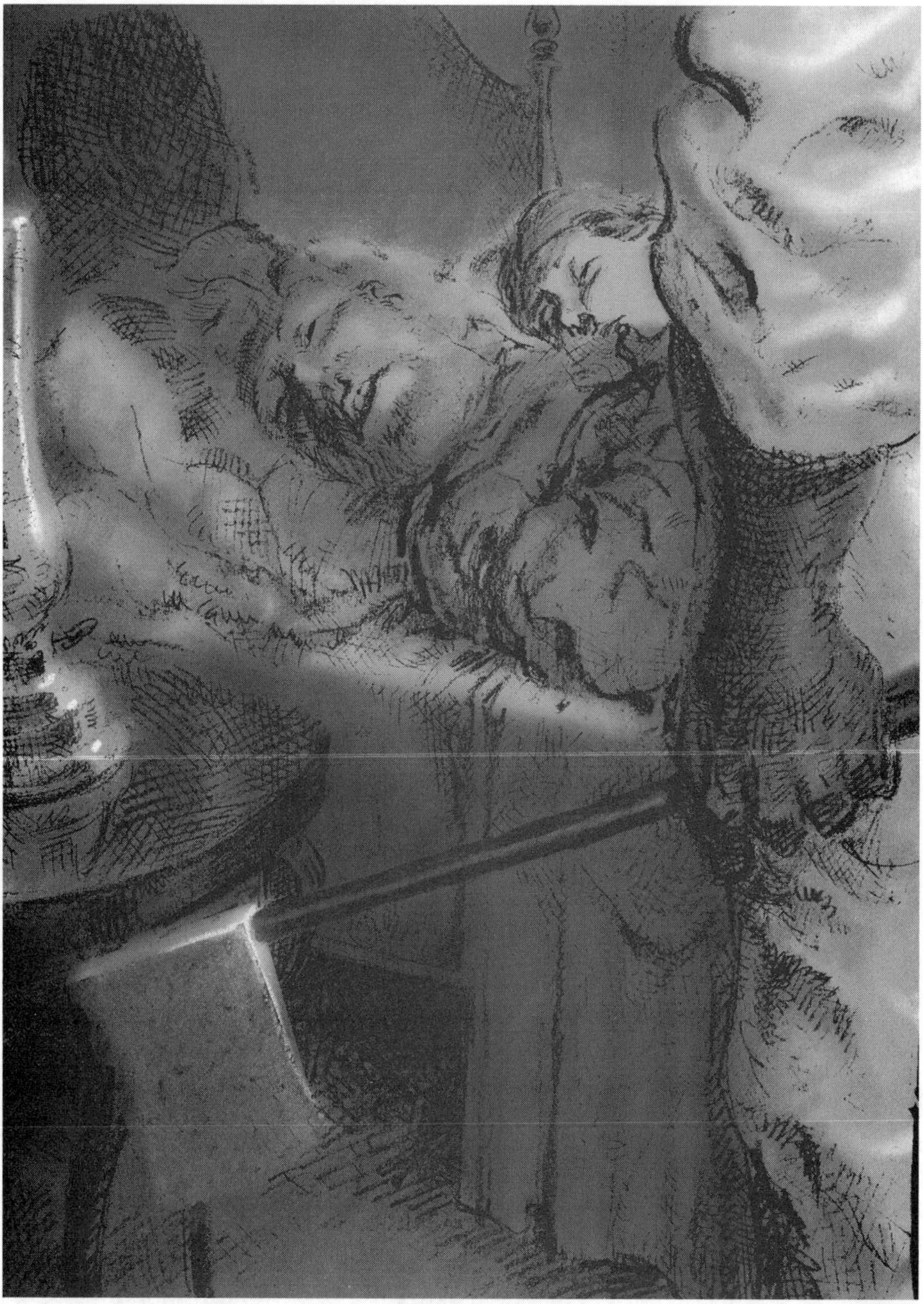

"IT WAS THEN OBSERVED THAT I MUST SPILL THE FIRST BLOOD. ON WHICH ARMED WITH A HATCHET, AND ACCOMPANIED BY WILL, I ENTERED MY MASTER'S CHAMBER;

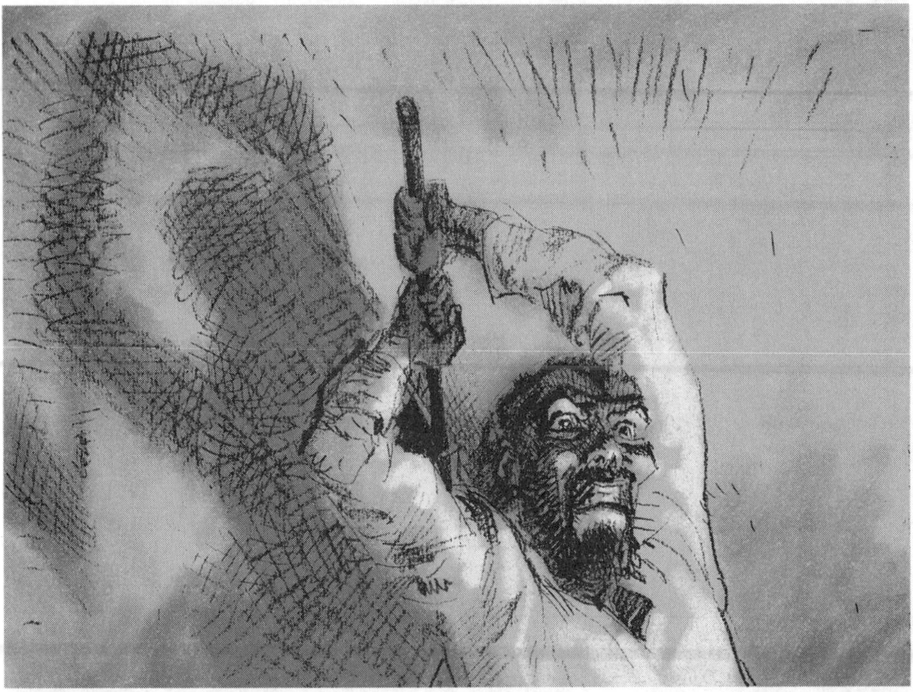

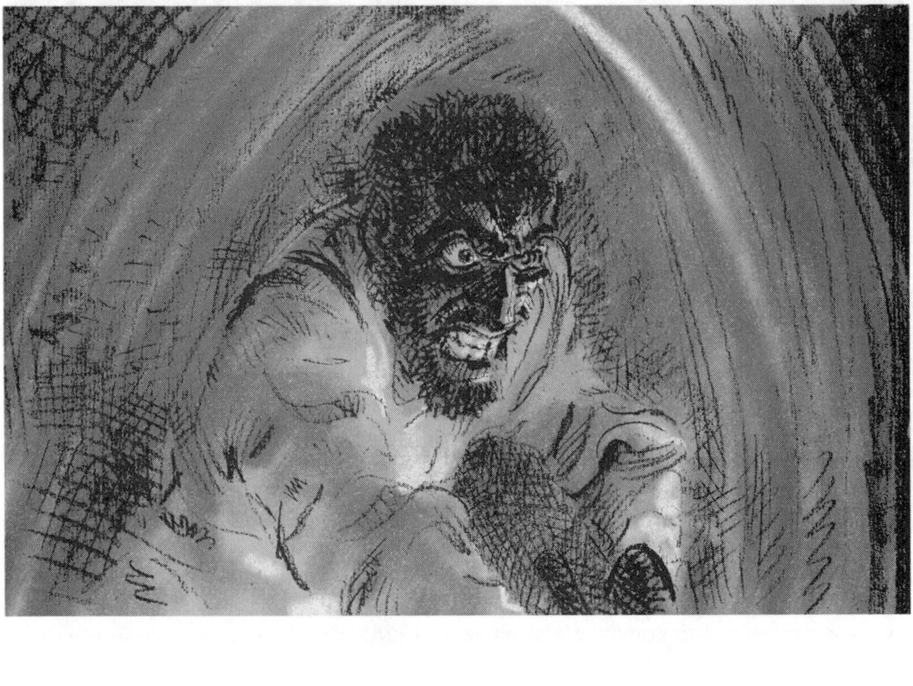

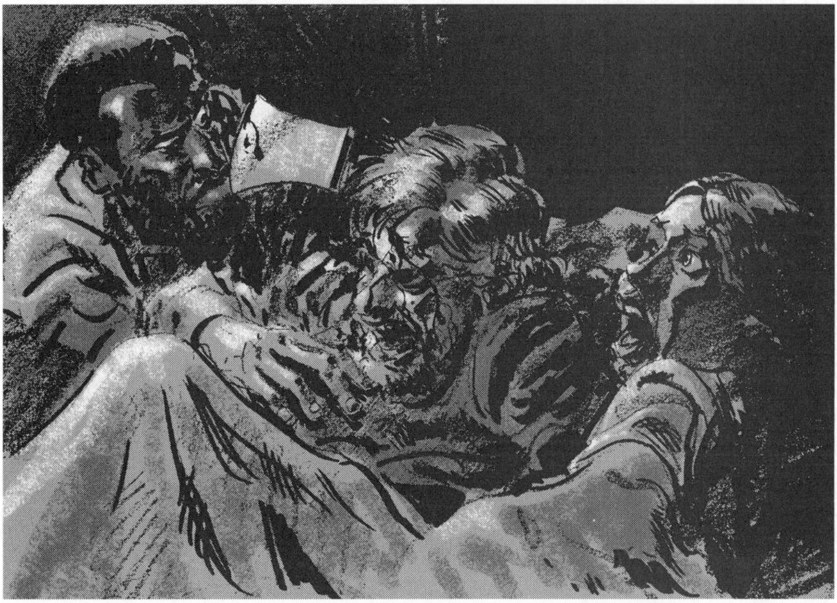

"It being dark, I could not give a death blow, the hatchet glanced from his head, he sprang from the bed and called his wife, it was his last word. Will laid him dead, with a blow of his axe, and Mrs. Travis shared the same fate.

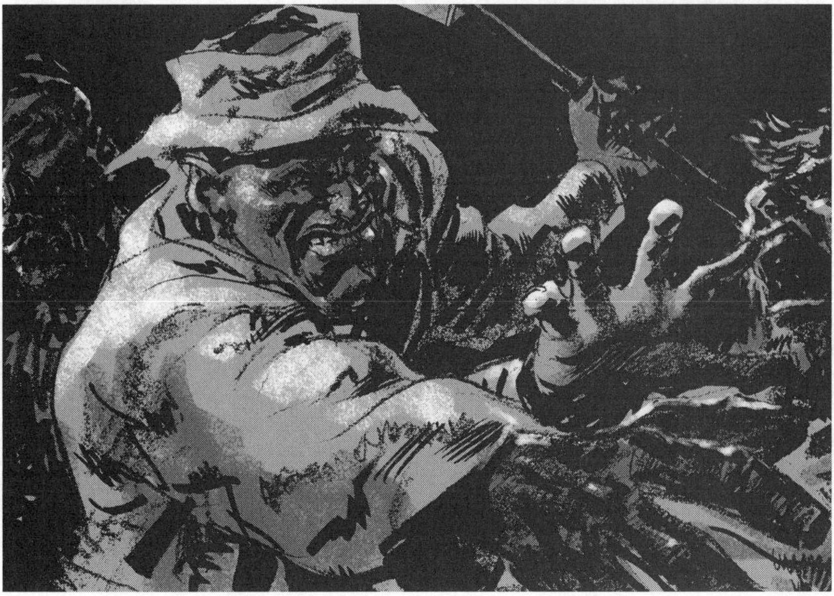

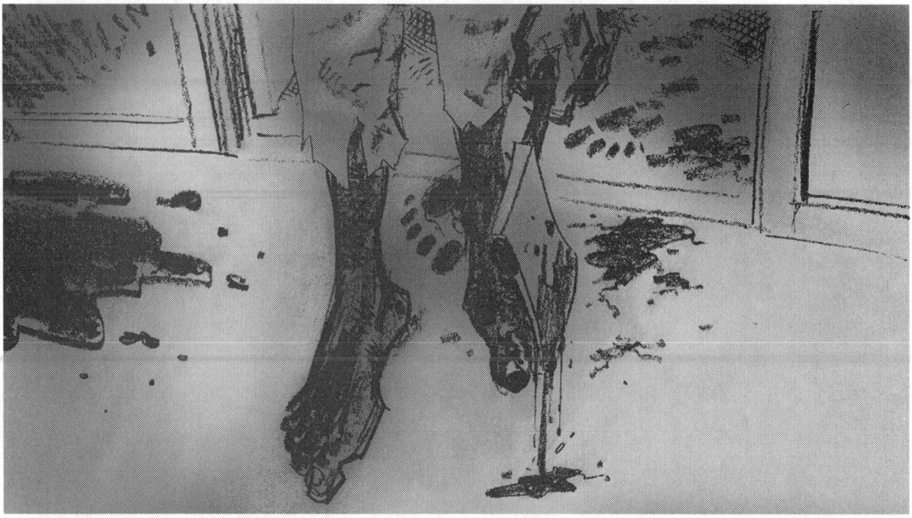

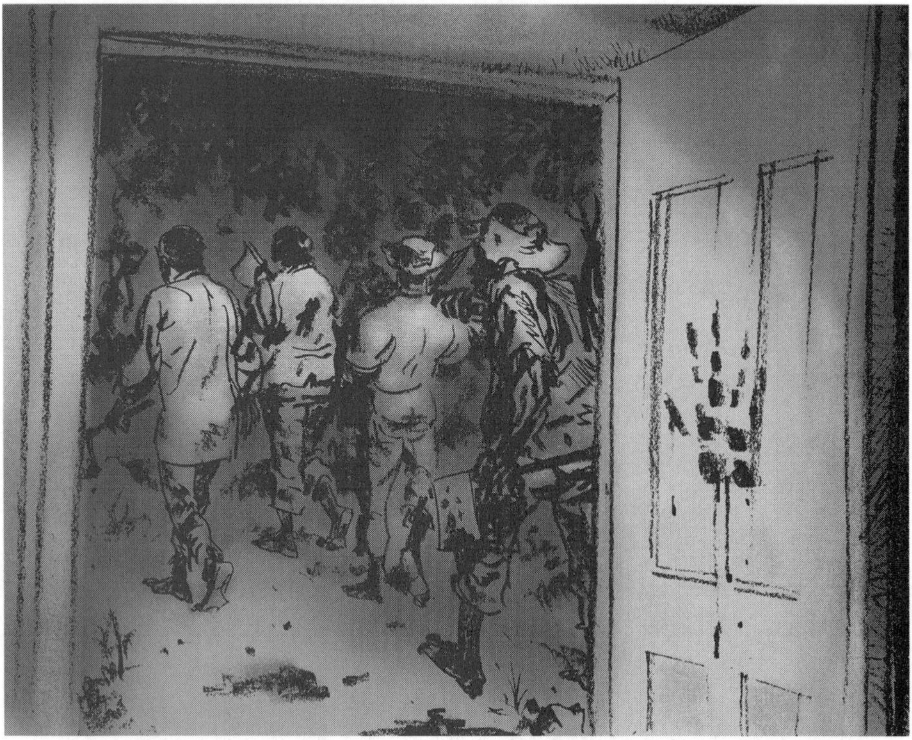

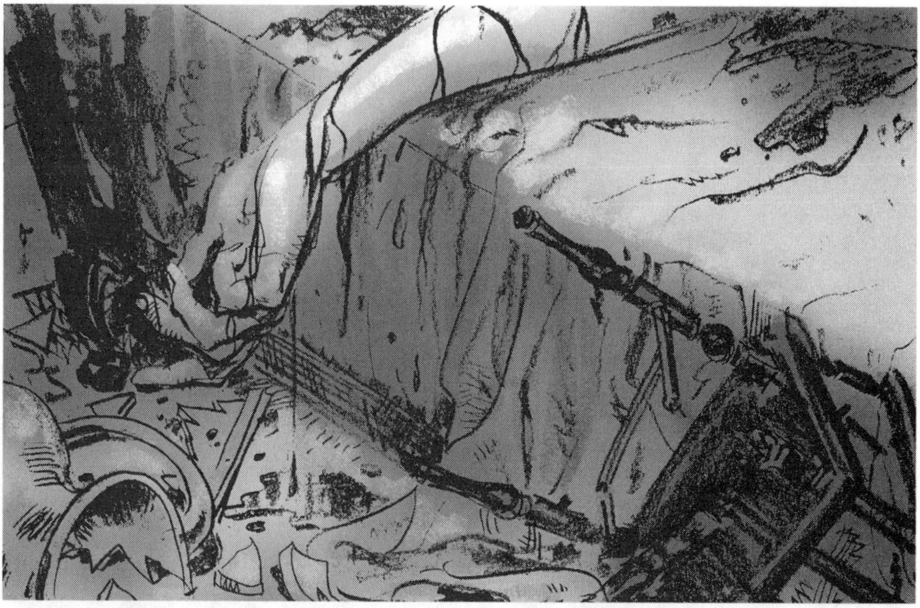

"THE MURDER OF THIS FAMILY FIVE IN NUMBER, WAS THE WORK OF A MOMENT.

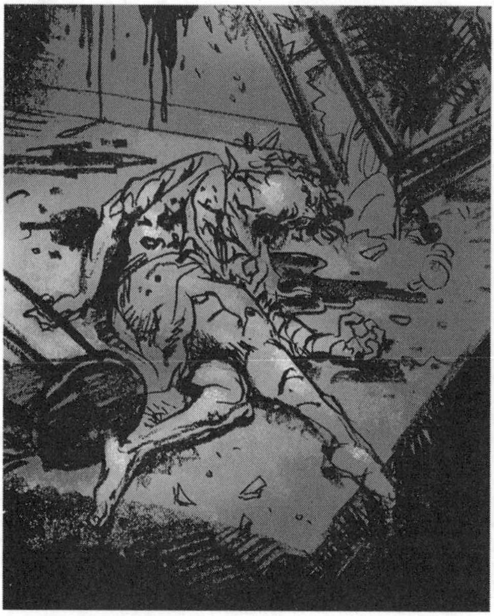

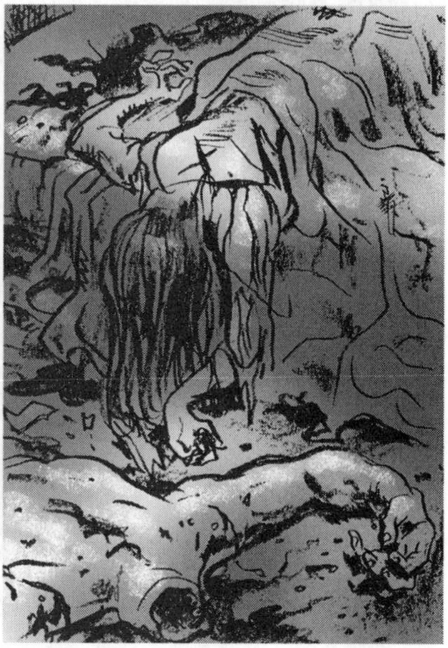

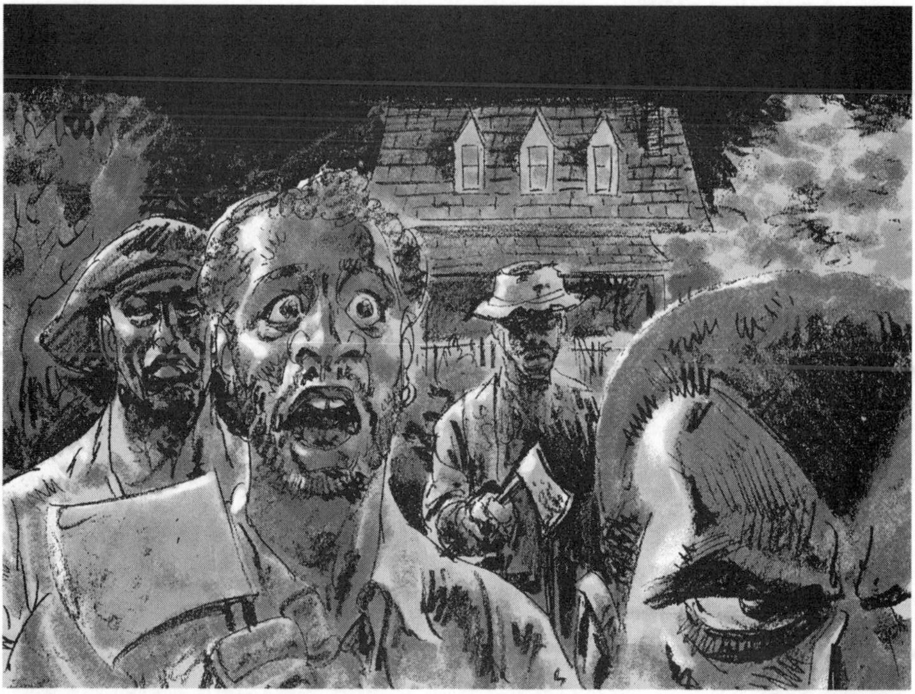

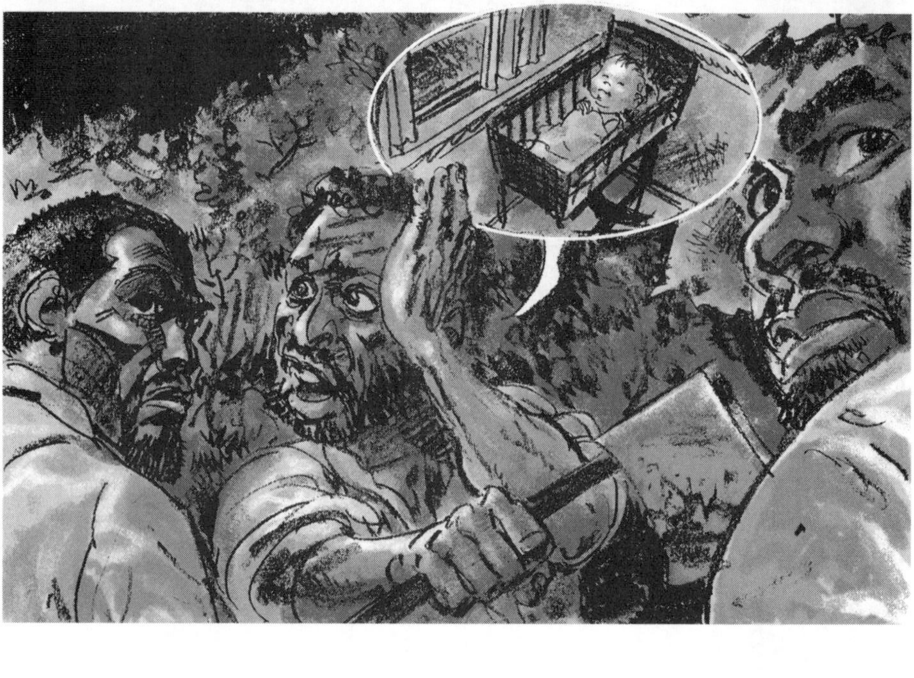

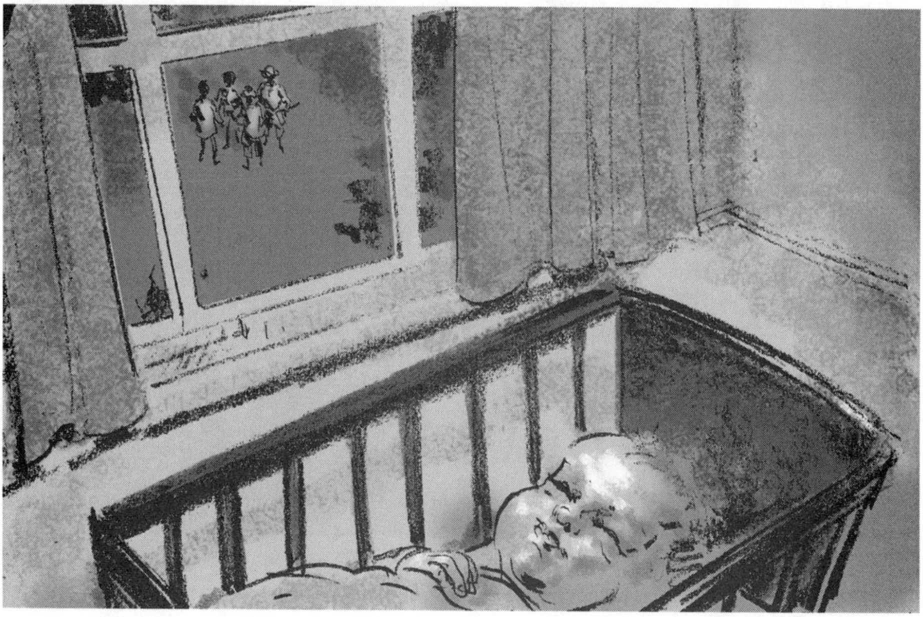

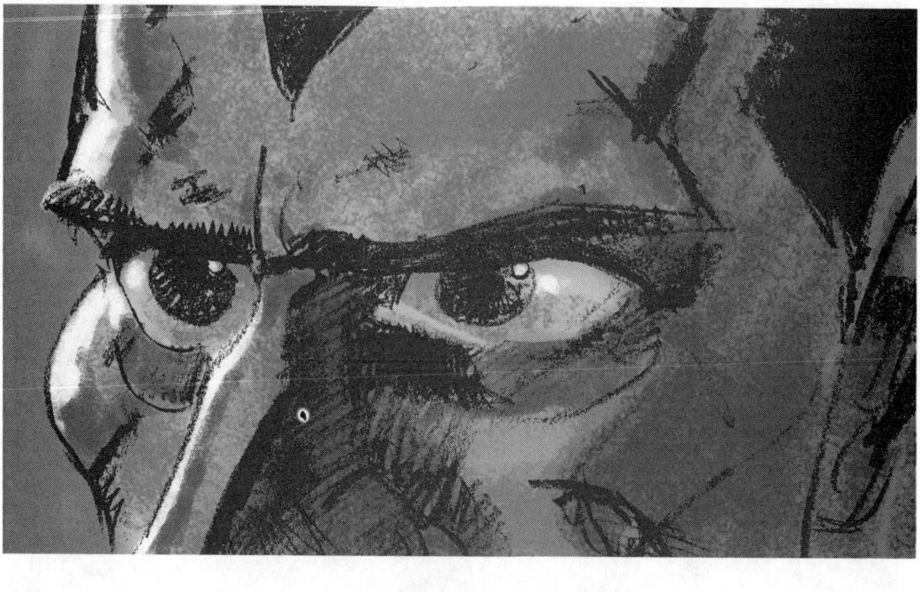

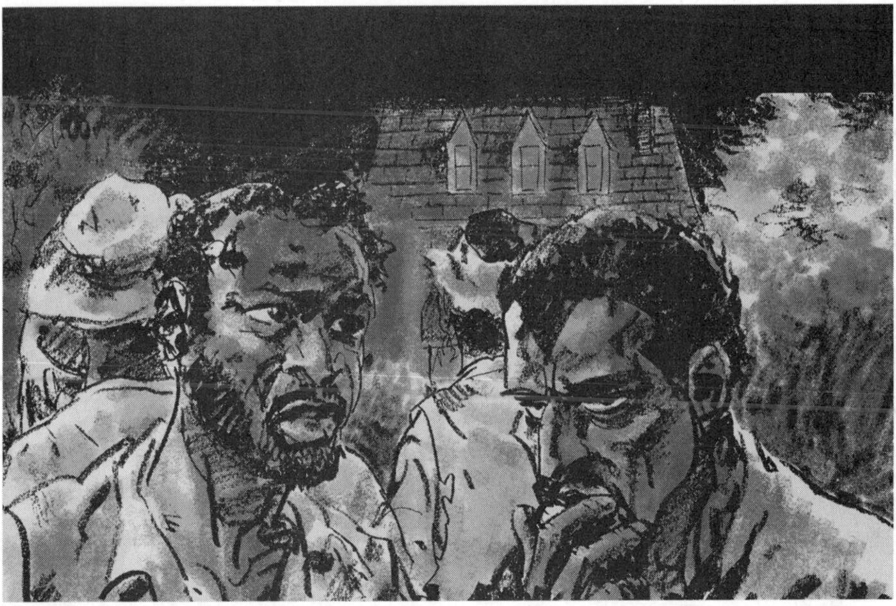

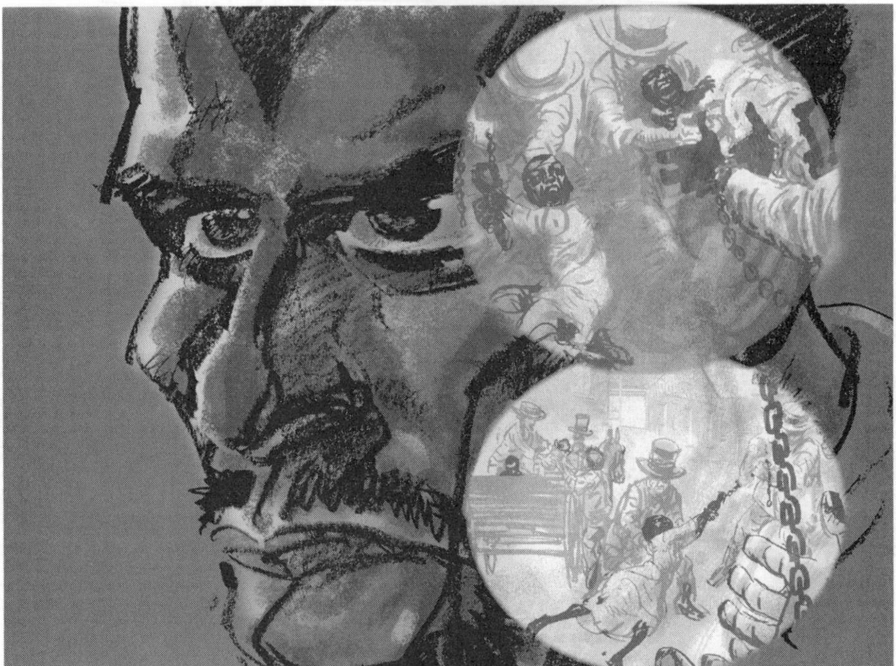

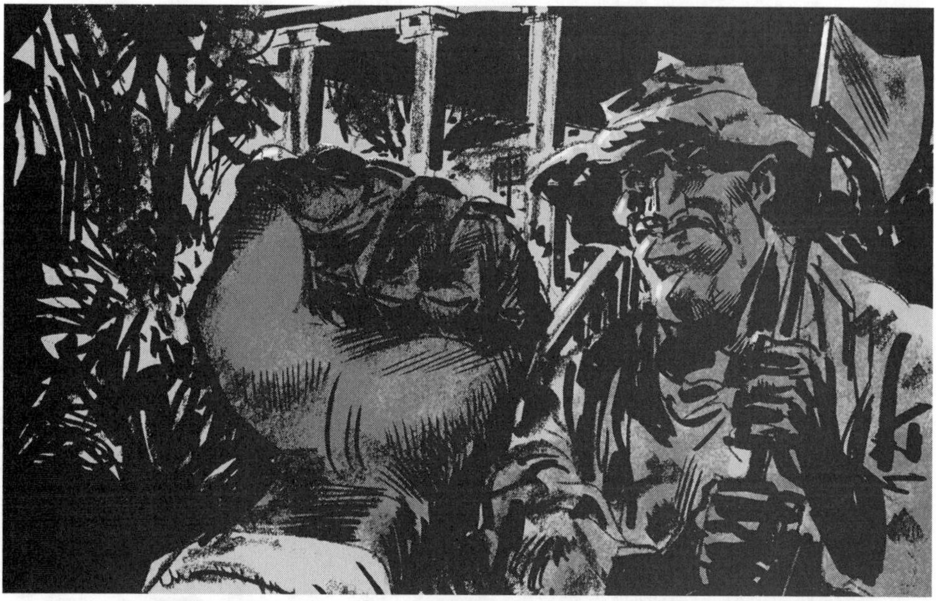

"THERE WAS A LITTLE INFANT SLEEPING IN A CRADLE, THAT WAS FORGOTTEN, UNTIL WE HAD LEFT THE HOUSE AND GONE SOME DISTANCE, WHEN HENRY AND WILL RETURNED AND KILLED IT;

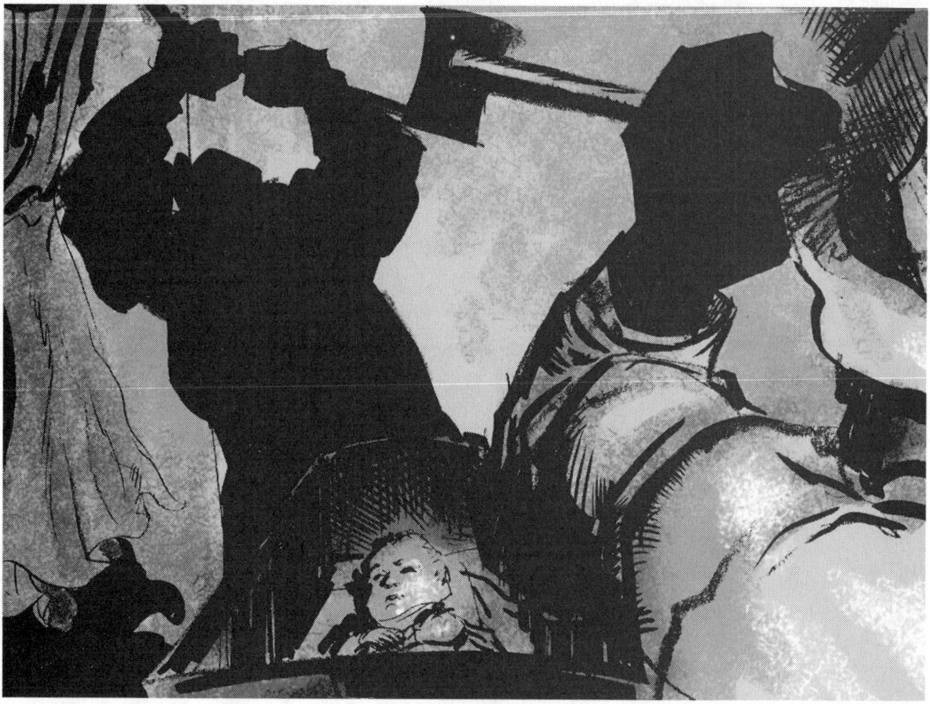

"WE GOT HERE, FOUR GUNS THAT WOULD SHOOT, AND
SEVERAL OLD MUSKETS, WITH A POUND OR TWO OF POWDER.

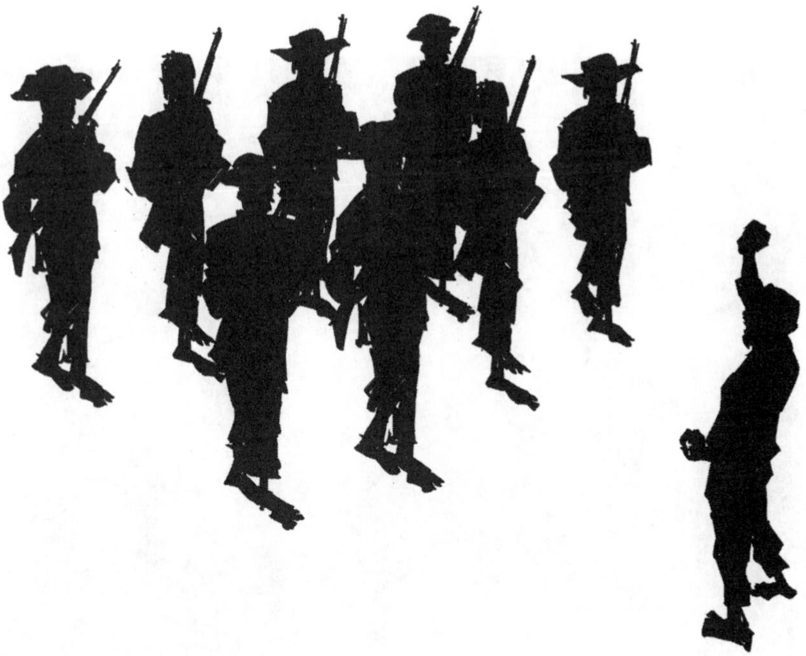

"WE REMAINED SOME TIME AT THE BARN, WHERE WE PARADED; I FORMED THEM IN A LINE AS SOLDIERS, AND AFTER CARRYING THEM THROUGH ALL THE MANOEUVRES I WAS MASTER OF, MARCHED THEM OFF TO MR. SALATHUL FRANCIS', ABOUT SIX HUNDRED YARDS DISTANT.

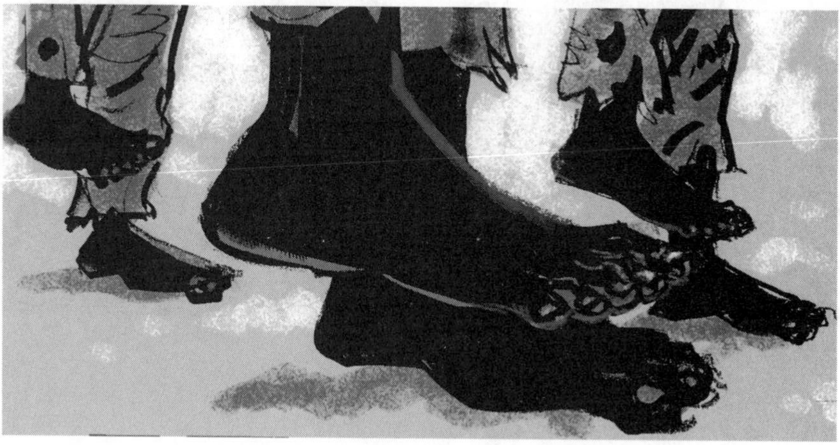

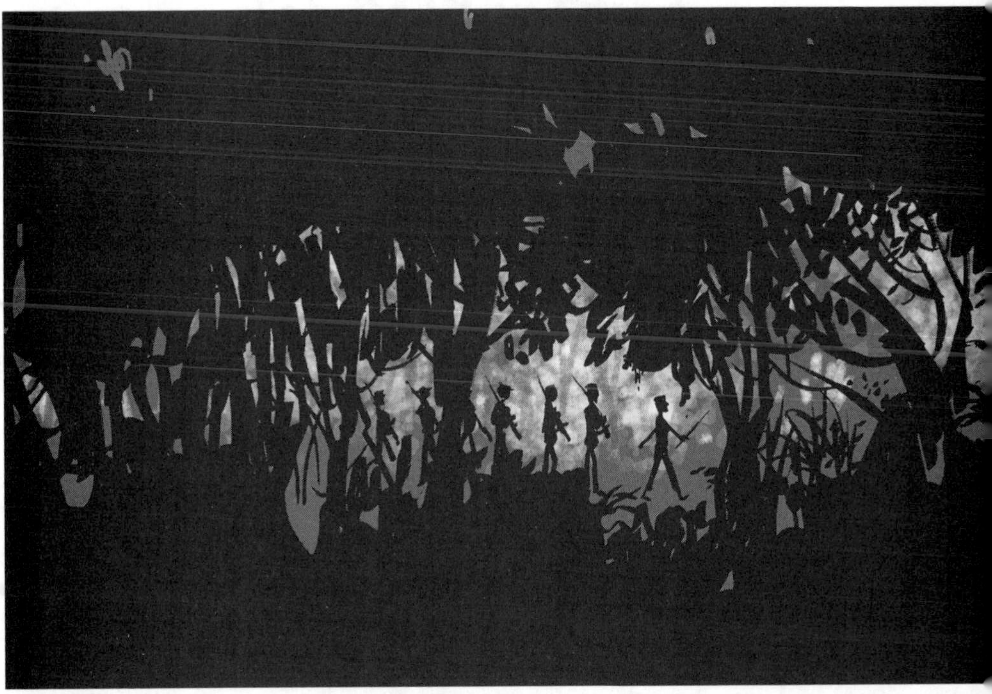

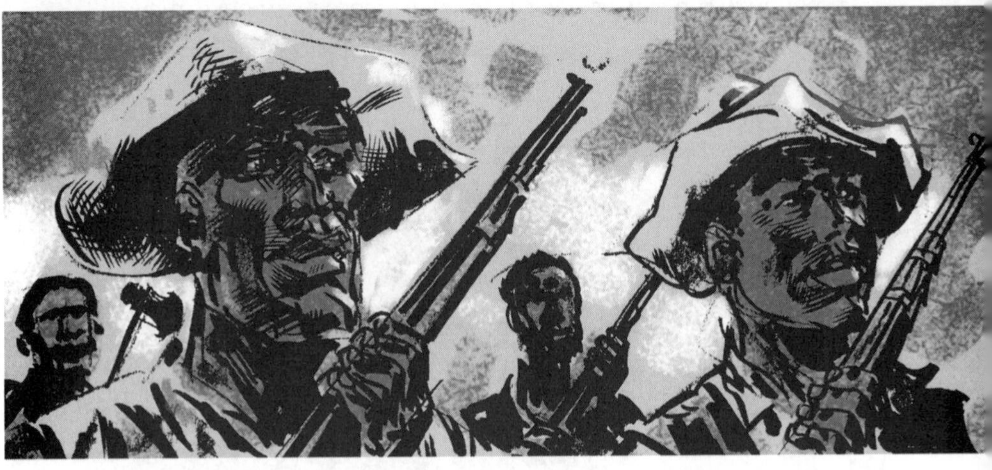

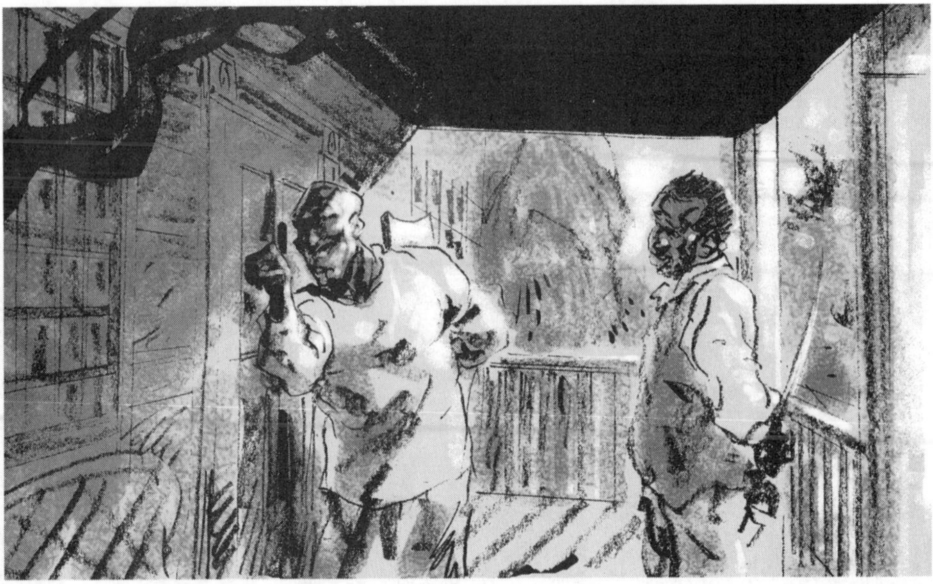

"SAM AND WILL WENT TO THE DOOR AND KNOCKED. MR. FRANCIS ASKED WHO WAS THERE, SAM REPLIED IT WAS HIM, AND HE HAD A LETTER FOR HIM, ON WHICH HE GOT UP AND CAME TO THE DOOR;

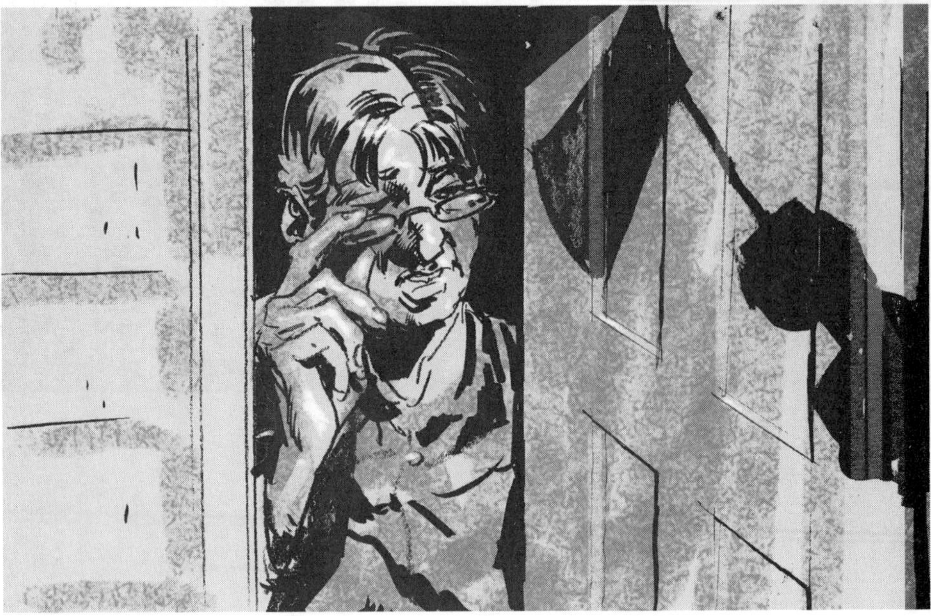

"THEY IMMEDIATELY SEIZED HIM, AND DRAGGING HIM OUT A LITTLE FROM THE DOOR, HE WAS DISPATCHED BY REPEATED BLOWS ON THE HEAD; THERE WAS NO OTHER WHITE PERSON IN THE FAMILY.

"WE STARTED FROM THERE FOR MRS. REESE'S, MAINTAINING THE MOST PERFECT SILENCE ON OUR MARCH, WHERE FINDING THE

DOOR UNLOCKED, WE ENTERED, AND MURDERED MRS. REESE IN HER BED, WHILE SLEEPING; HER SON AWOKE, BUT IT WAS ONLY TO SLEEP THE SLEEP OF DEATH, HE HAD ONLY TIME TO SAY WHO IS THAT, AND HE WAS NO MORE. FROM MRS. REESE'S WE WENT TO MRS. TURNER'S, A MILE DISTANT, WHICH WE REACHED ABOUT SUNRISE, ON MONDAY MORNING. HENRY, AUSTIN, AND SAM, WENT TO THE STILL, WHERE, FINDING MR. PEEBLES, AUSTIN SHOT HIM, AND THE REST OF US WENT TO

THE HOUSE; AS WE APPROACHED, THE FAMILY DISCOVERED US, AND SHUT THE DOOR. VAIN HOPE! WILL, WITH ONE STROKE OF HIS

AXE, OPENED IT, AND WE ENTERED AND FOUND MRS. TURNER AND MRS. NEWSOME IN THE MIDDLE OF A ROOM ALMOST FRIGHTENED TO DEATH. WILL IMMEDIATELY KILLED MRS. TURNER, WITH ONE BLOW OF HIS AXE. I TOOK MRS. NEWSOME BY THE HAND, AND WITH THE SWORD I HAD WHEN I WAS APPREHENDED, I STRUCK HER SEVERAL BLOWS OVER THE HEAD, BUT NOT BEING ABLE TO KILL HER, AS THE SWORD WAS DULL. WILL TURNING AROUND AND DISCOVERING IT, DISPATCHED HER ALSO.

"A GENERAL DESTRUCTION OF PROPERTY AND SEARCH FOR MONEY AND AMMUNITION, ALWAYS SUCCEEDED THE MURDERS.

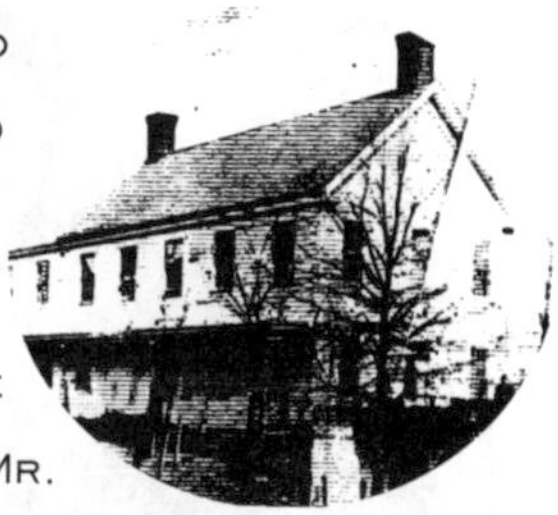

"By this time my company amounted to fifteen, and nine men mounted, who started for Mrs. Whitehead's, (the other six were to go through a by way to Mr. Bryant's, and rejoin us at Mrs. Whitehead's,) as we approached the house we discovered Mr. Richard Whitehead standing in the cotton patch, near

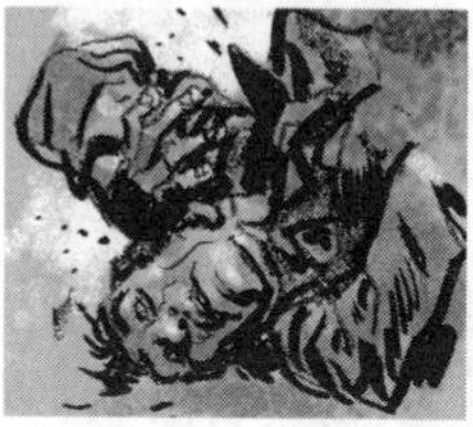

the lane fence; we called him over into the lane, and Will, the executioner, was near at hand, with his fatal axe, to send him to an untimely grave. As we pushed on to the house, I discovered some one run round the garden, and thinking it

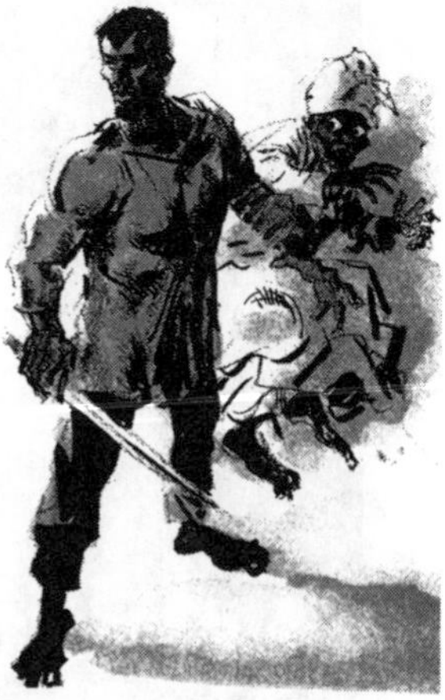

was some of the white family, I pursued them, but finding it was a servant girl belonging to the house, I returned to commence the work of death, but they whom I left, had not been idle; all the family were already murdered, but Mrs. Whitehead and her daughter Margaret. As I came round to the door I saw Will pulling Mrs. Whitehead out of the house, and at the step he nearly severed her head from her body, with his broad axe. Miss Margaret, when I discovered her, had concealed herself in the corner, formed by the projection of the cellar cap

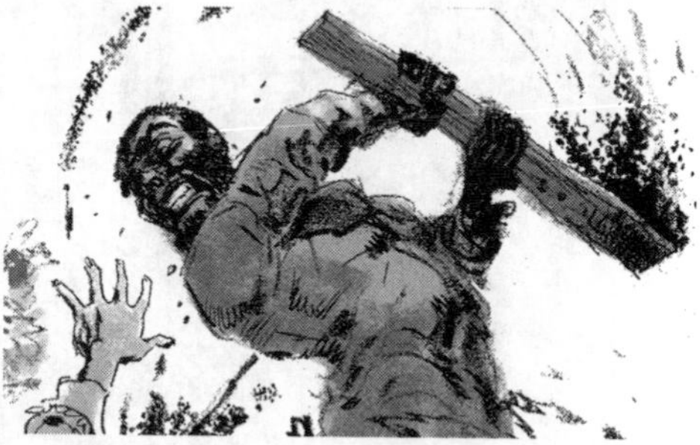

from the house; on my approach she fled, but was soon overtaken, and after repeated blows with a sword, I killed her by a blow on the head, with a fence rail. By this time, the six who had gone by Mr. Bryant's, rejoined us, and informed me they had done the work of death assigned them.

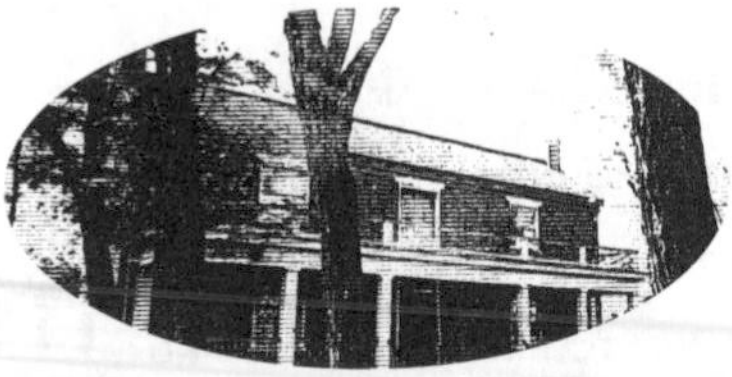

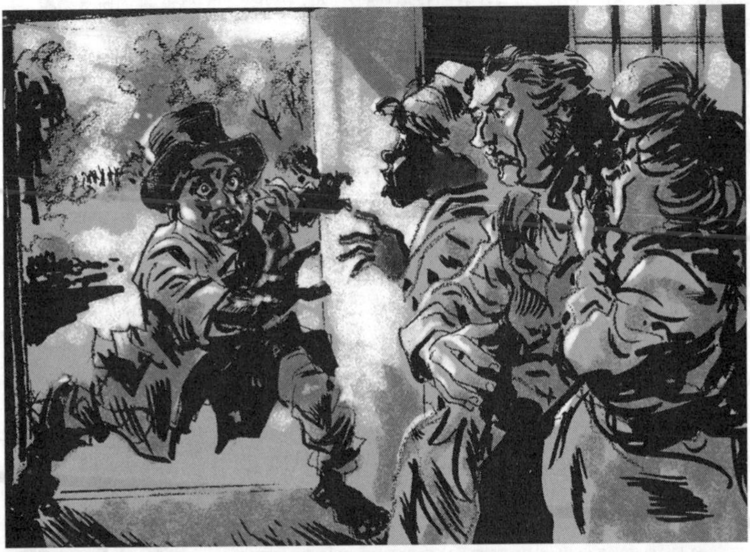

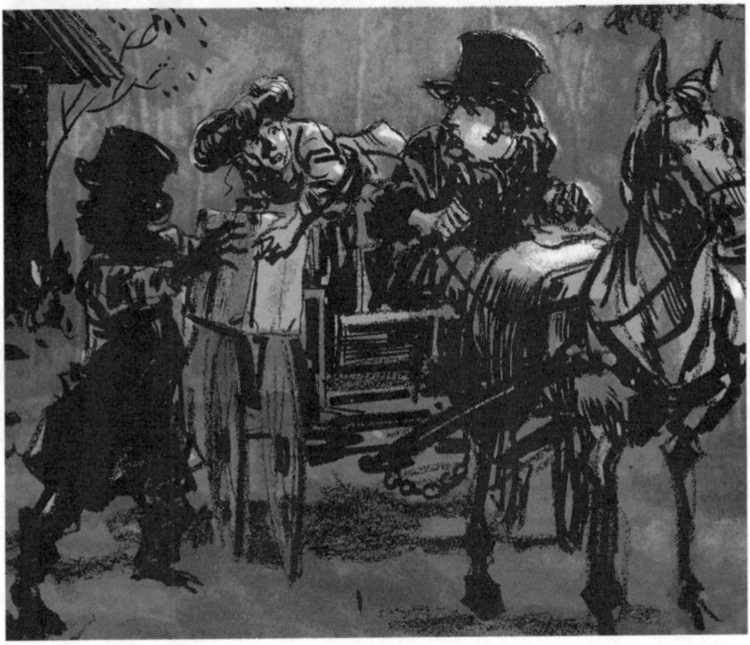

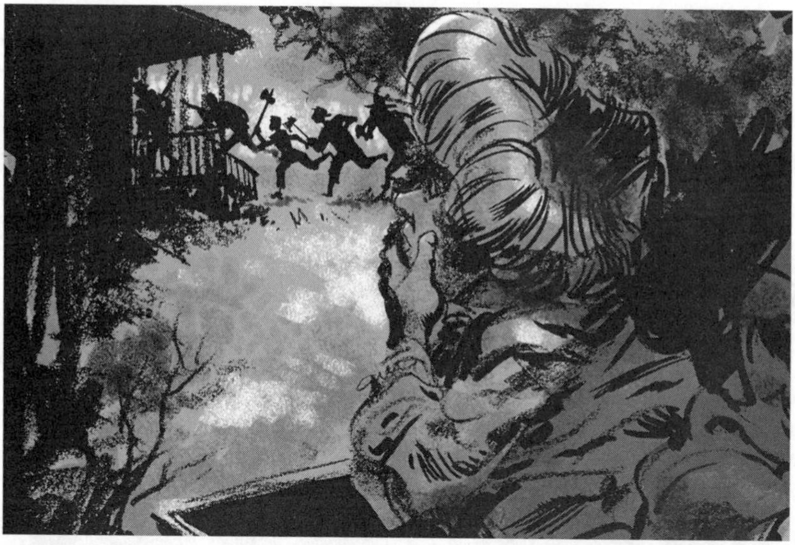

"We again divided, part going to Mr. Richard Porter's, and from thence to Nathaniel Francis', the others to Mr. Howell Harris', and Mr. T. Doyle's. On my reaching Mr. Porter's, he had escaped with his family. I understood there, that the alarm had already spread,

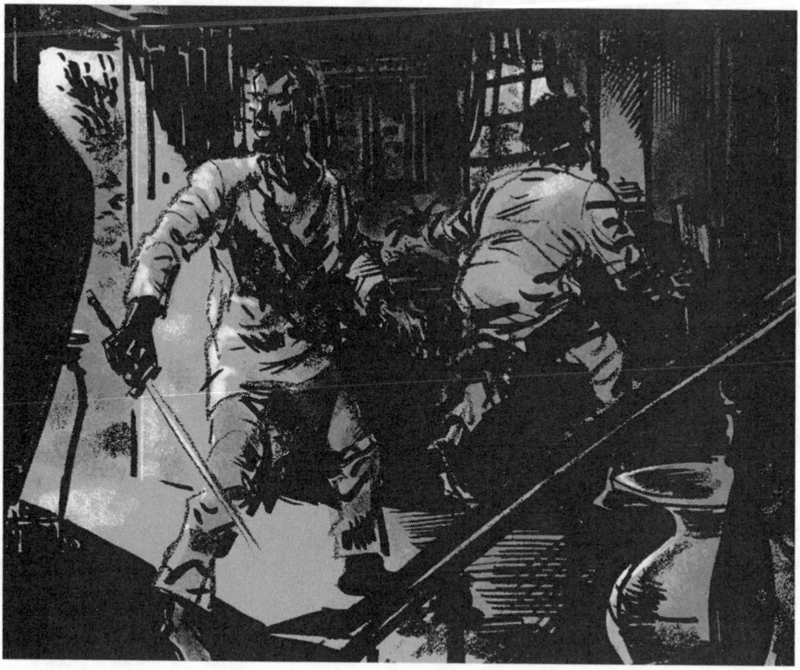

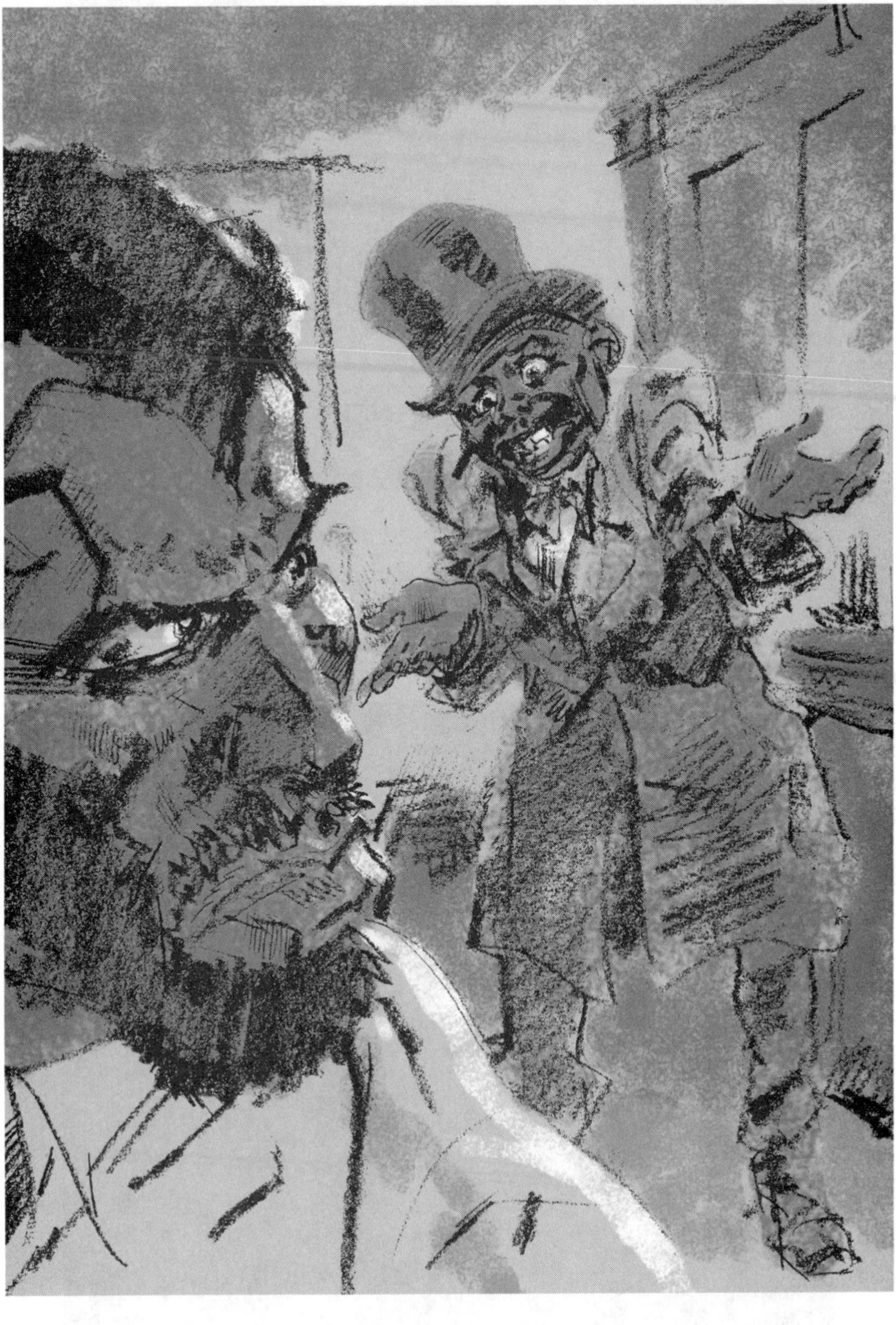

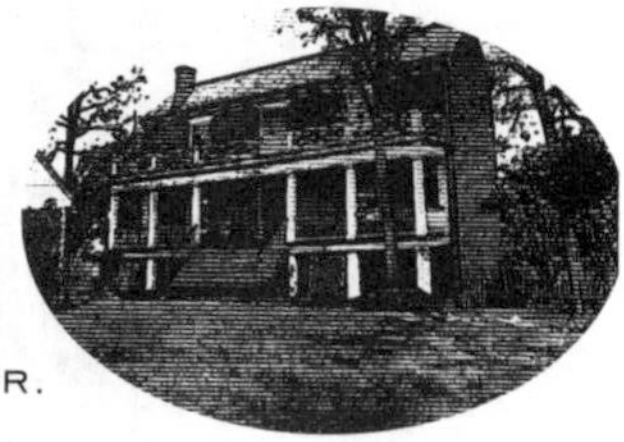

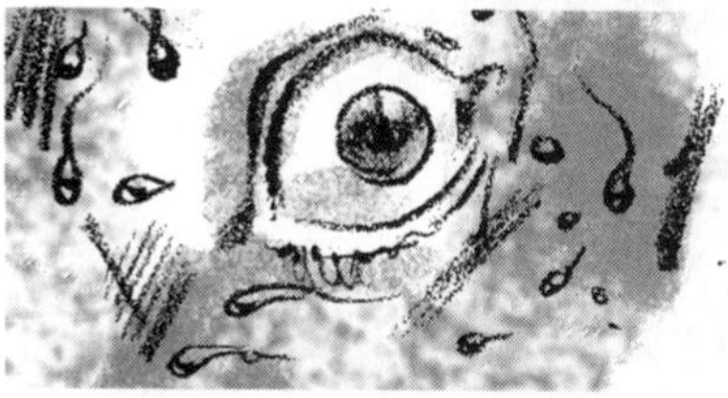

"I immediately returned to bring up those sent to Mr. Doyle's, and Mr. Howell Harris'; the party I left going on to Mr. Francis', having told them I would join them in that neighborhood. I met these sent to Mr. Doyle's and Mr. Harris' returning, having met Mr. Doyle on the road and killed him; and learning from some who joined them, that Mr. Harris was from home, I immediately pursued the course taken by the party gone on before; but knowing they would complete the work of death and pillage, at Mr. Francis' before I could get there, I went to Mr. Peter Edwards', expecting to find them there, but they had been here also. I then went to Mr. John T. Barrow's, they had been here and murdered him.

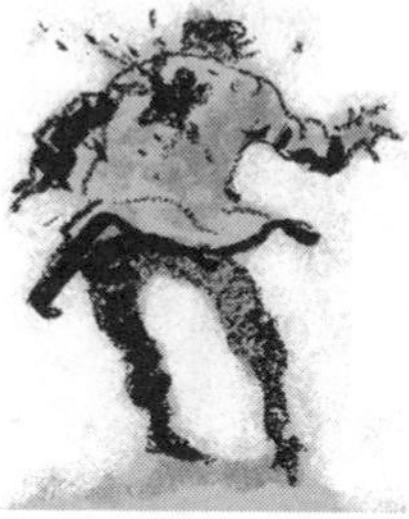

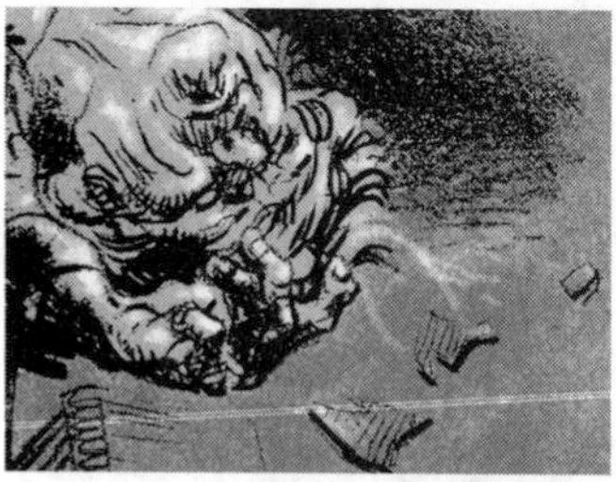

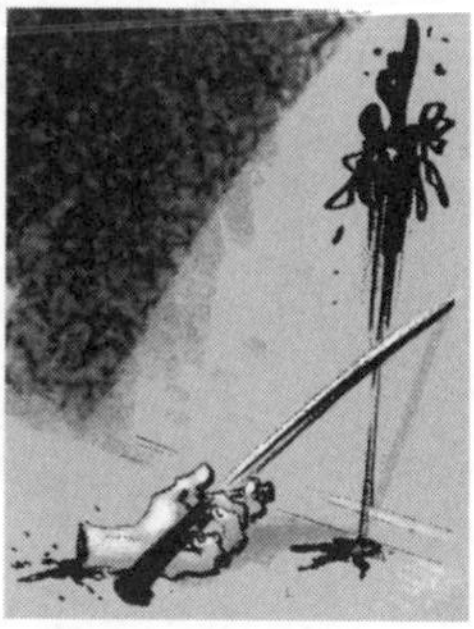

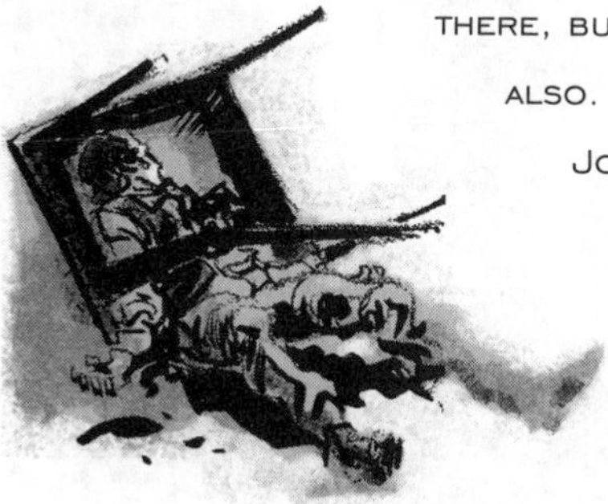

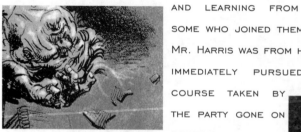

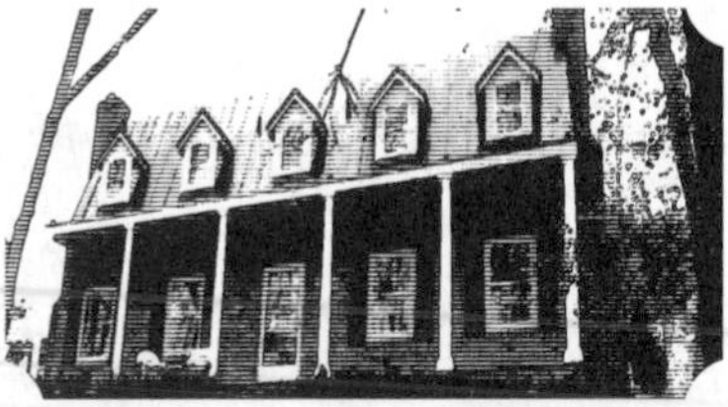

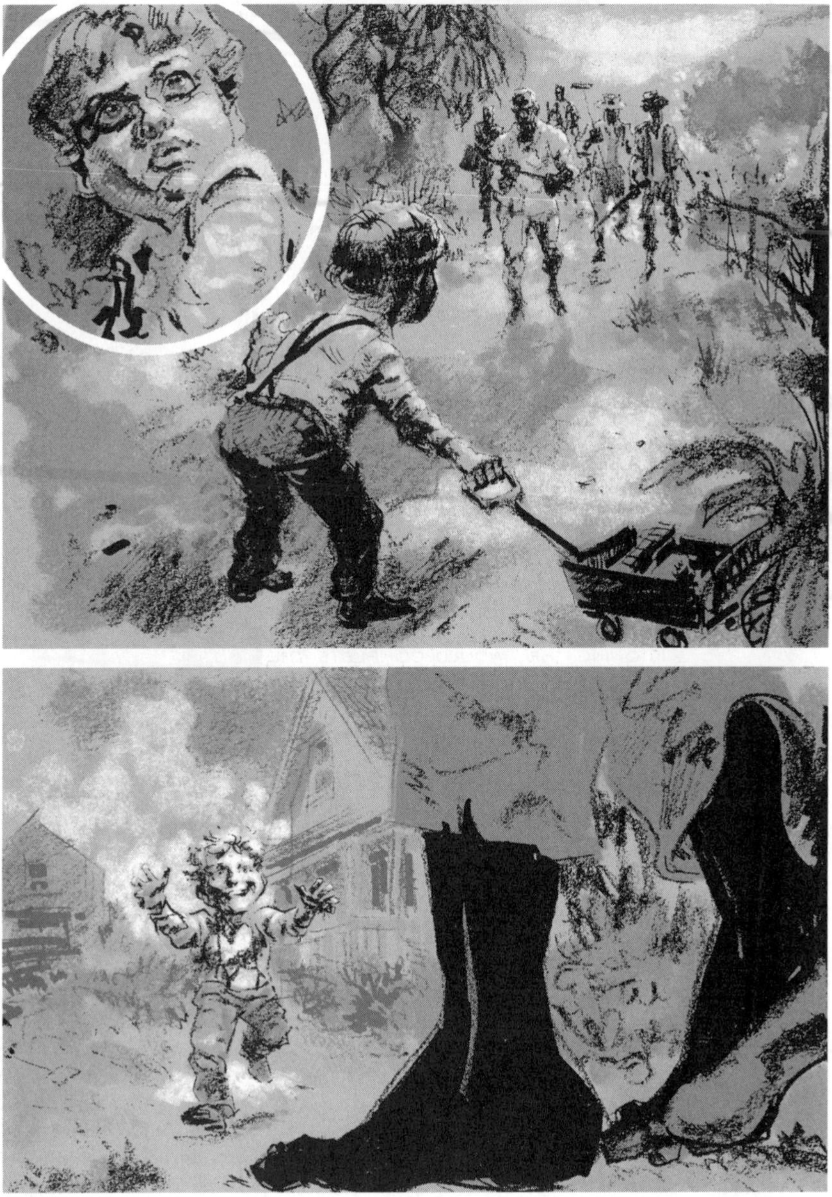

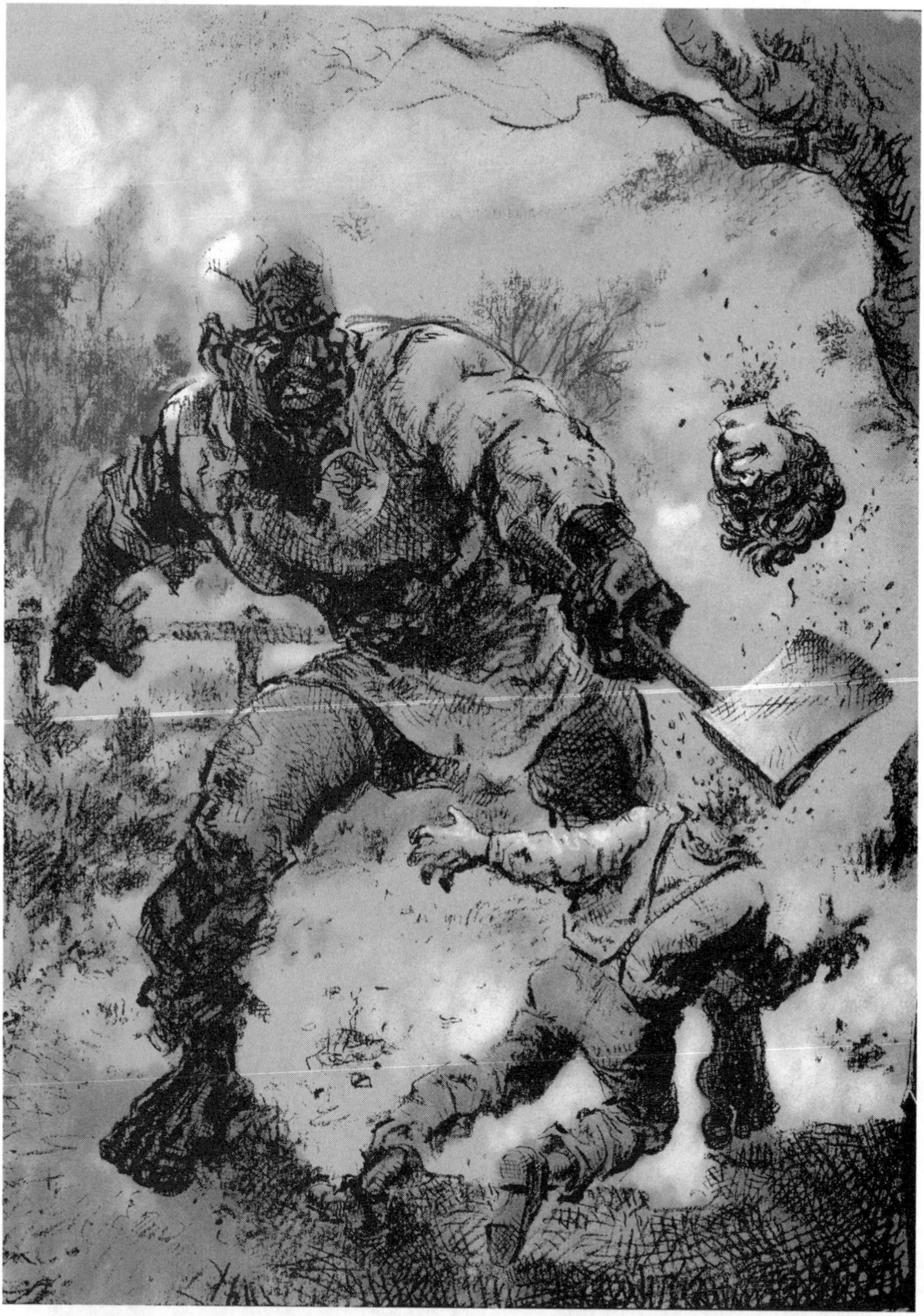

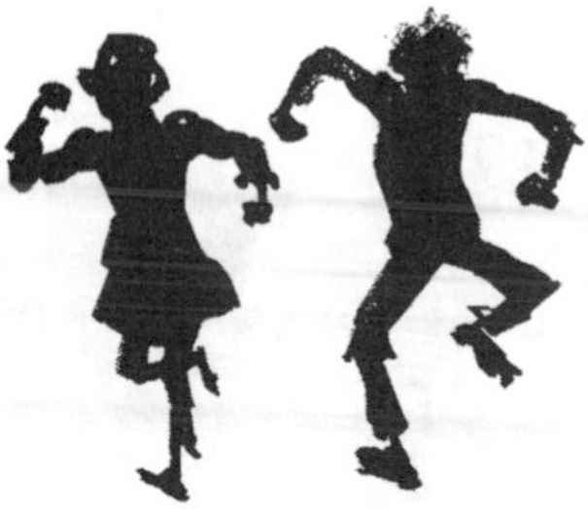

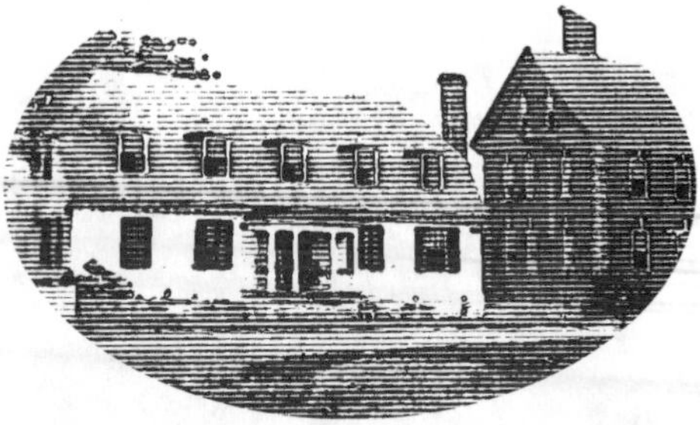

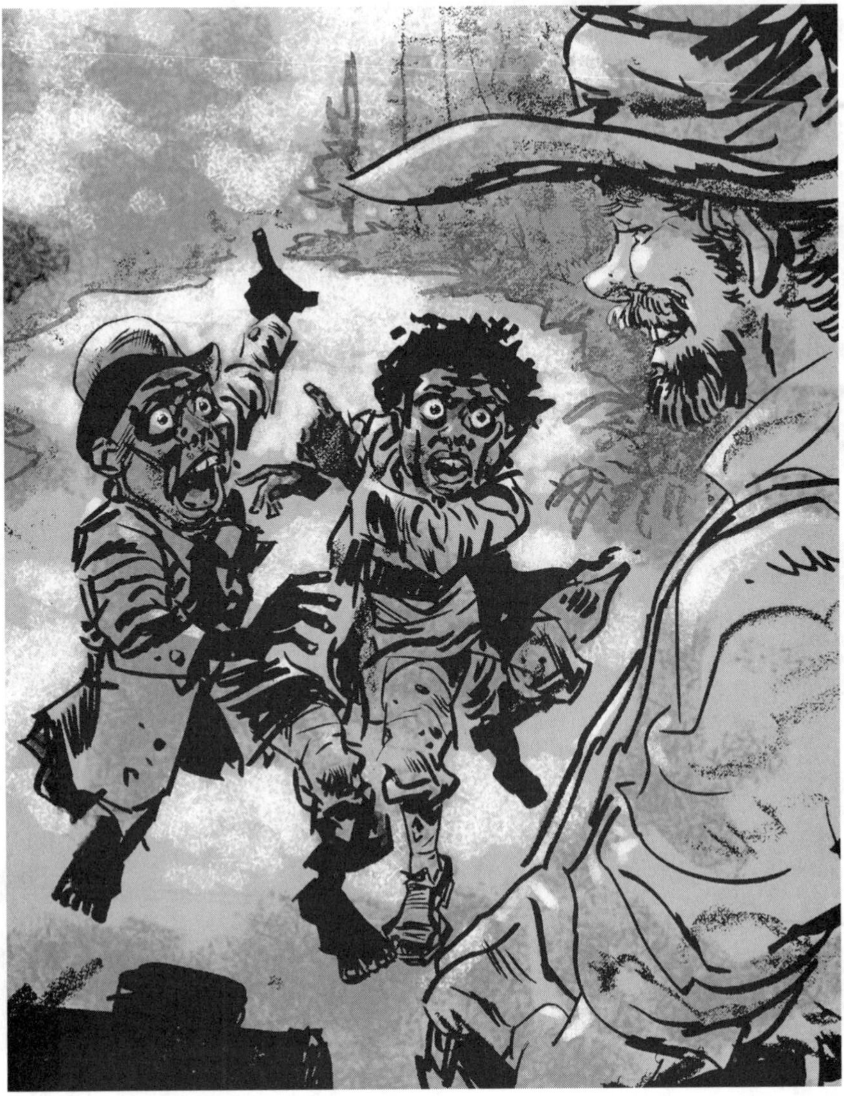

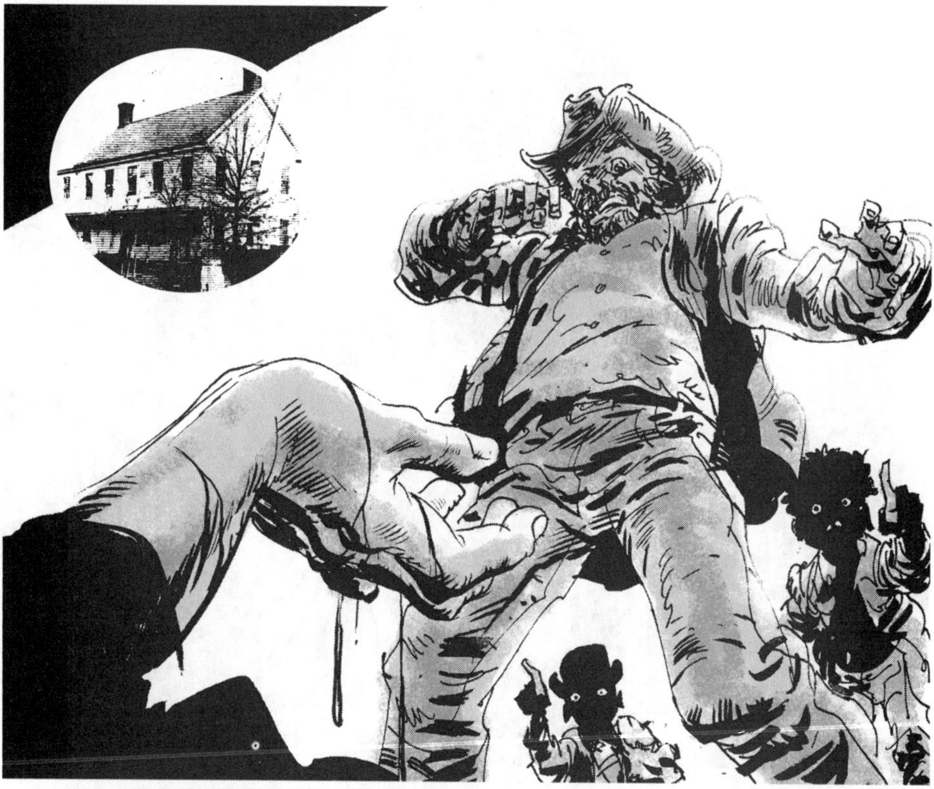

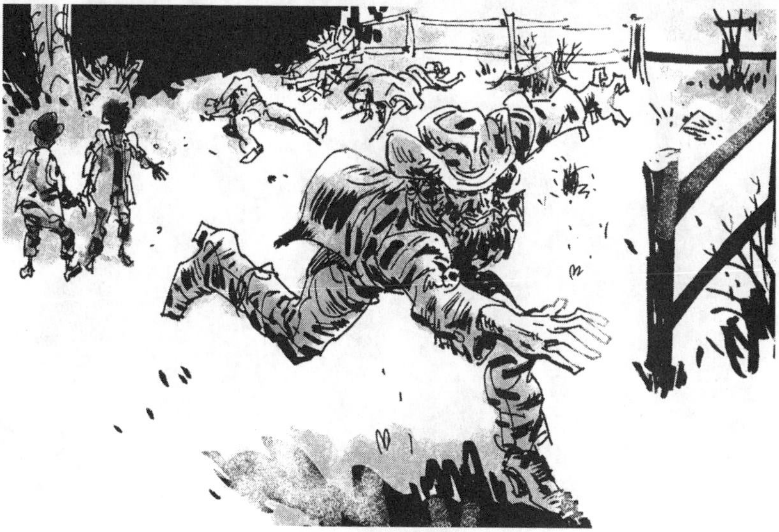

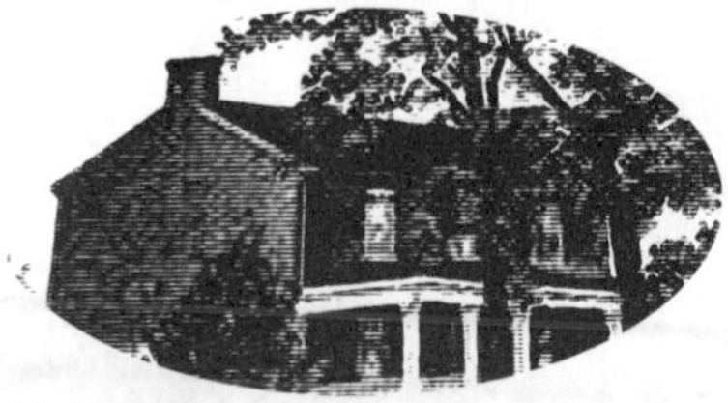

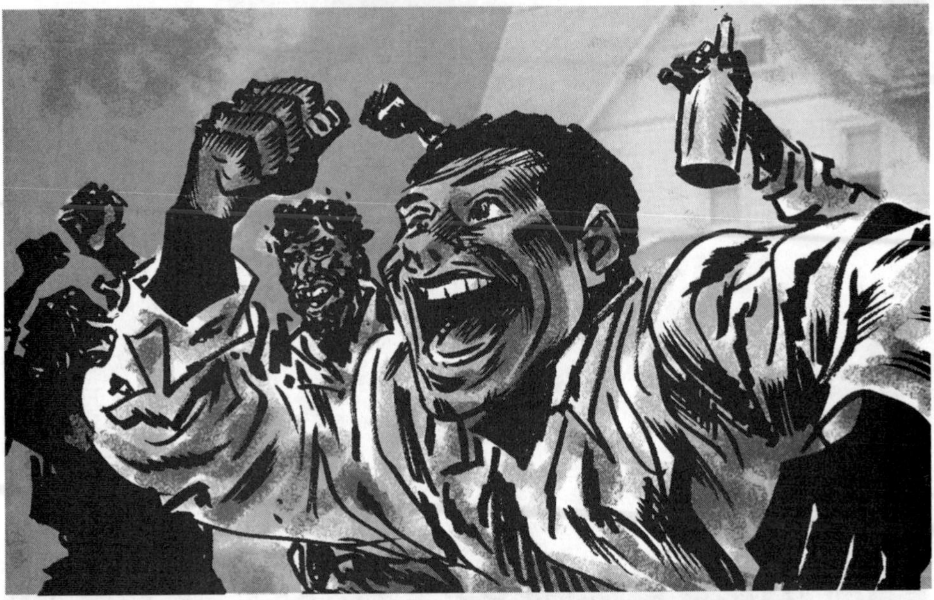

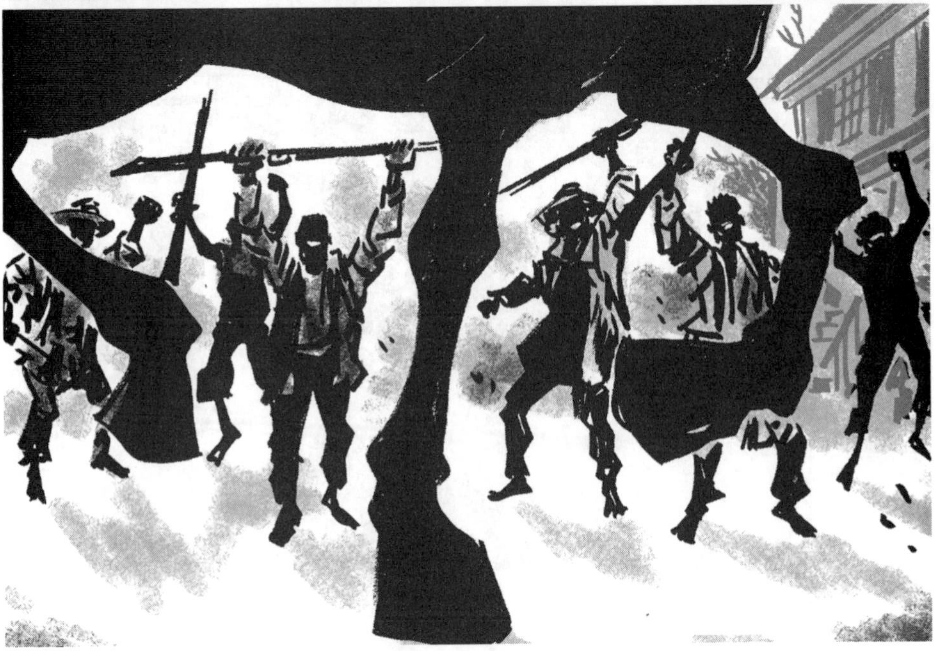

"I pursued on their track to Capt. Newit Harris', where I found the greater part mounted, and ready to start;

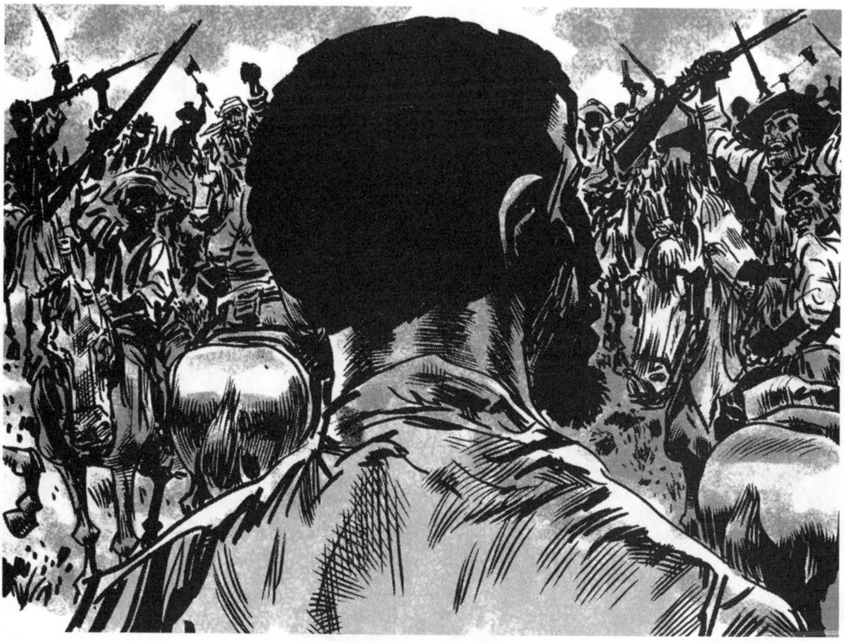

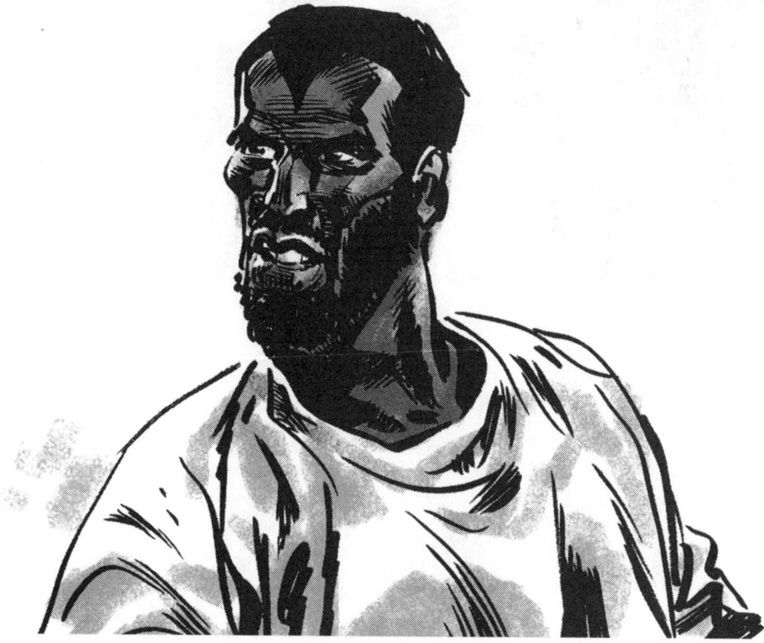

"THE MEN NOW AMOUNTING TO ABOUT FORTY, SHOUTED AND HURRAED AS I RODE UP, SOME WERE IN THE YARD, LOADING THEIR GUNS, OTHERS DRINKING.

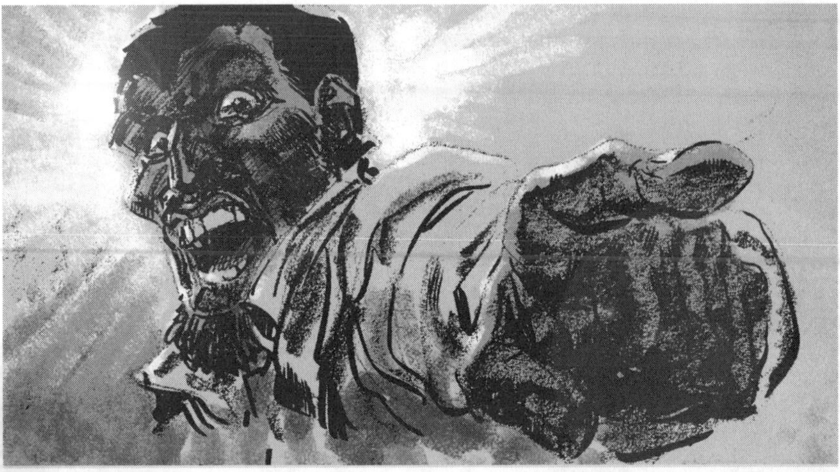

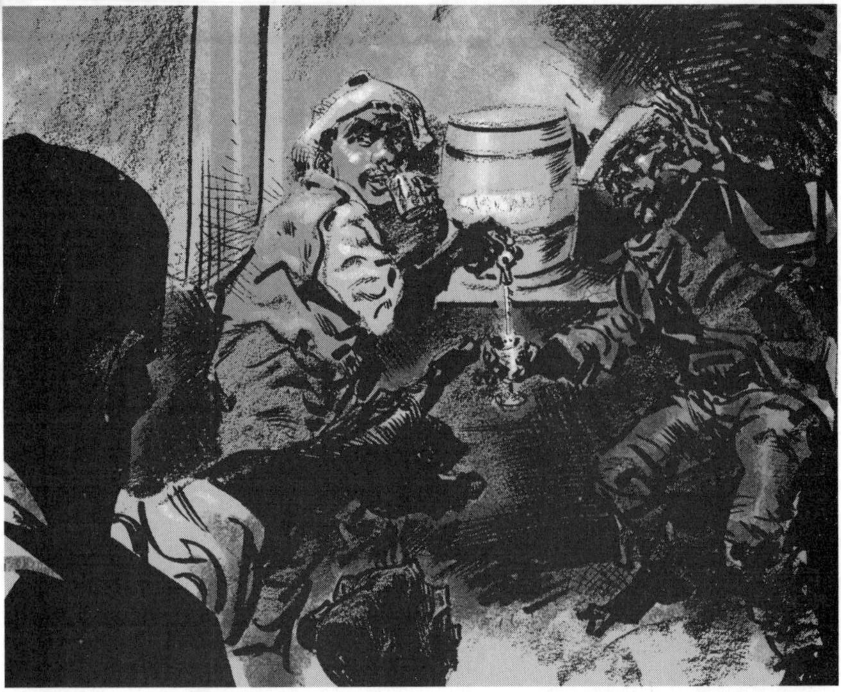

"They said Captain Harris and his family had escaped, the property in the house they destroyed, robbing him of money and other valuables. I ordered them to mount and march instantly, this was about nine or ten o'clock, Monday morning.

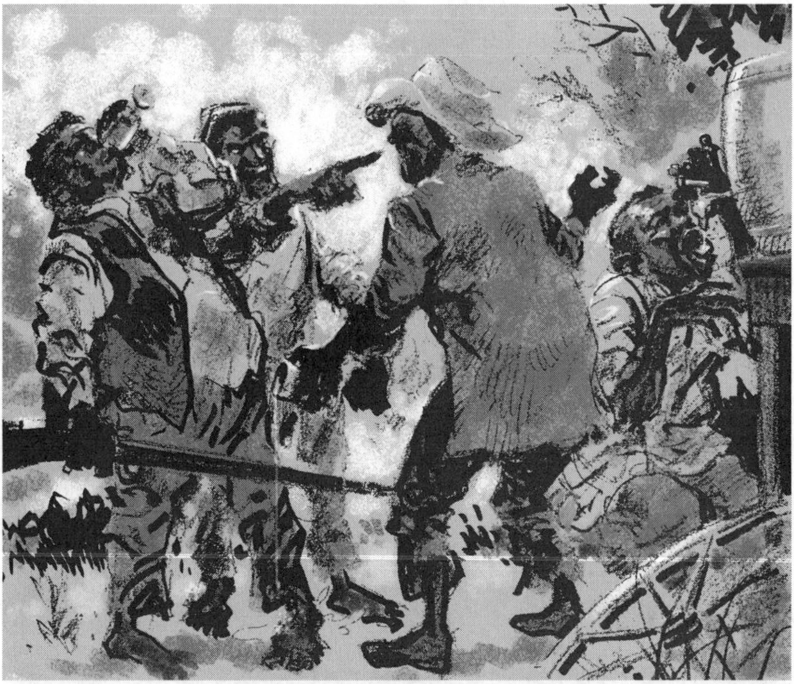

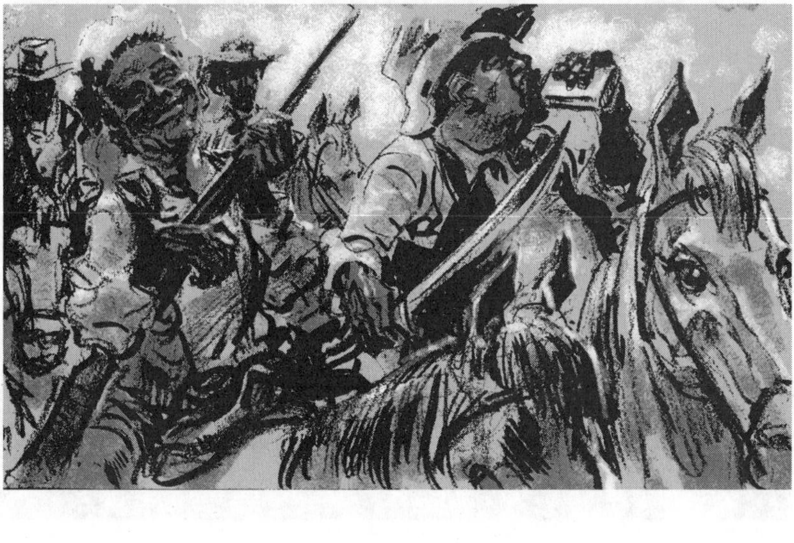

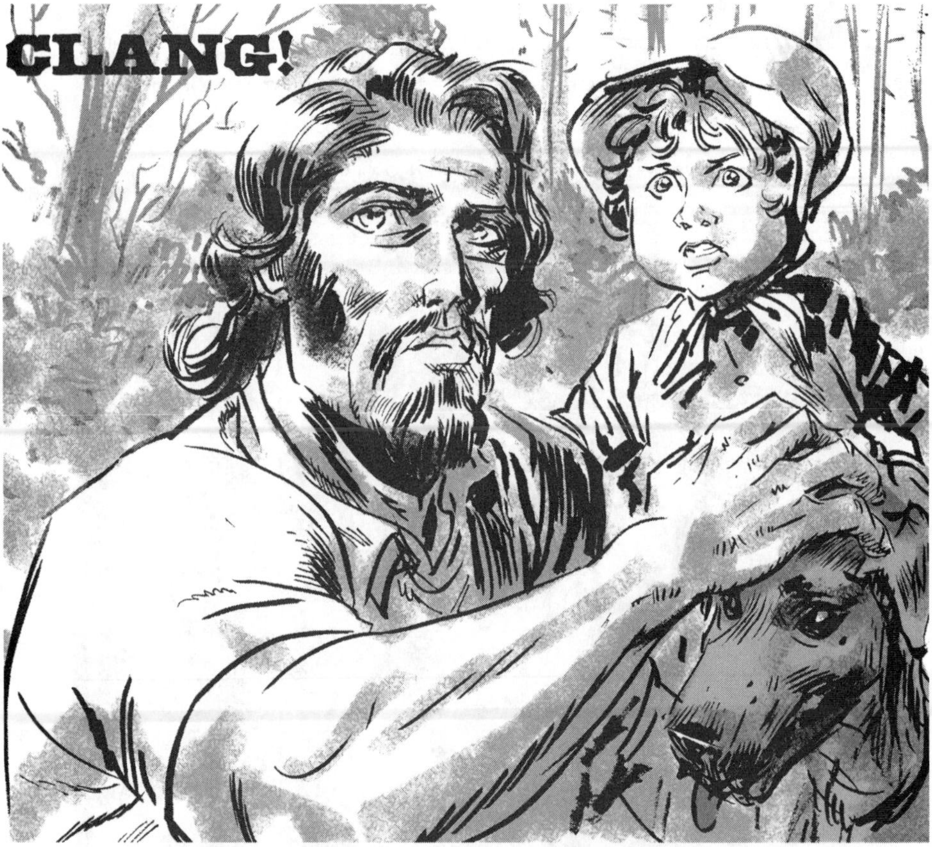
CLANG!

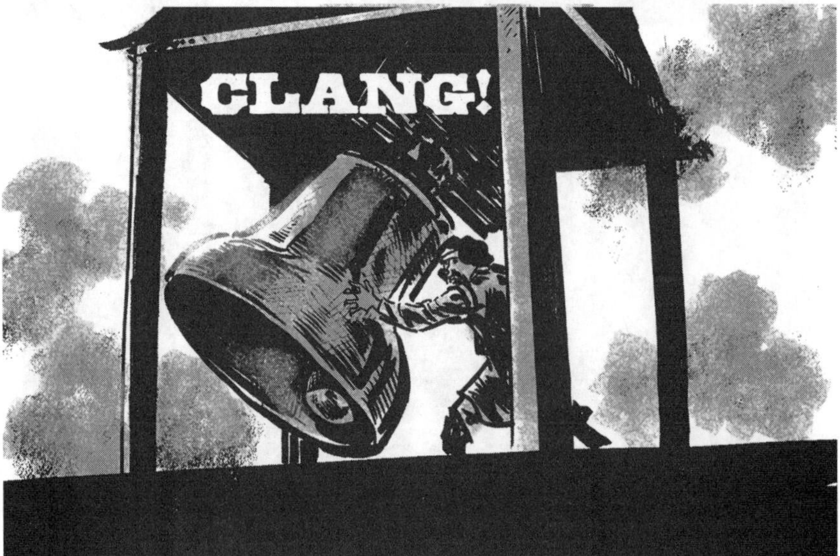
CLANG!

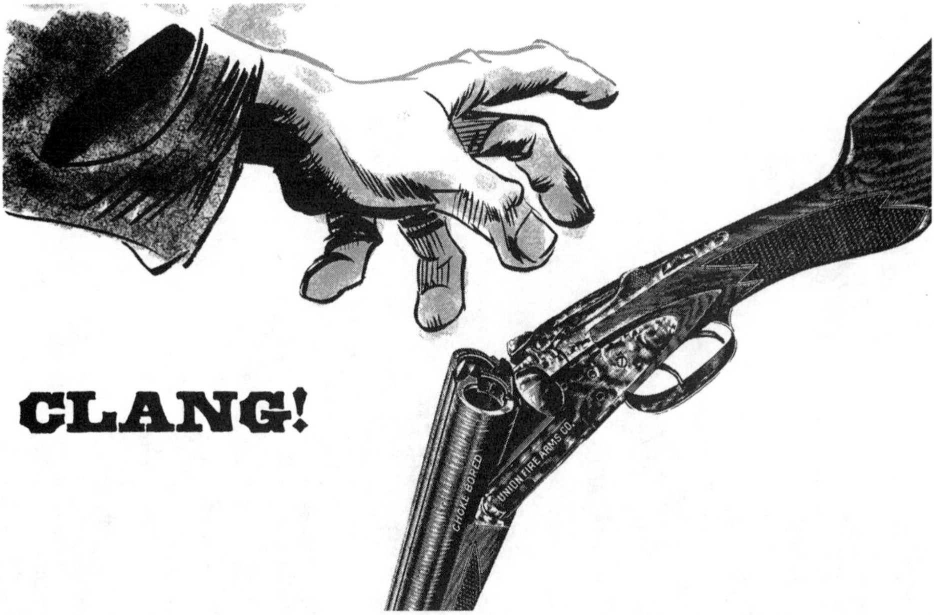
CLANG!
CHOKE BORED
UNION FIRE ARMS CO.

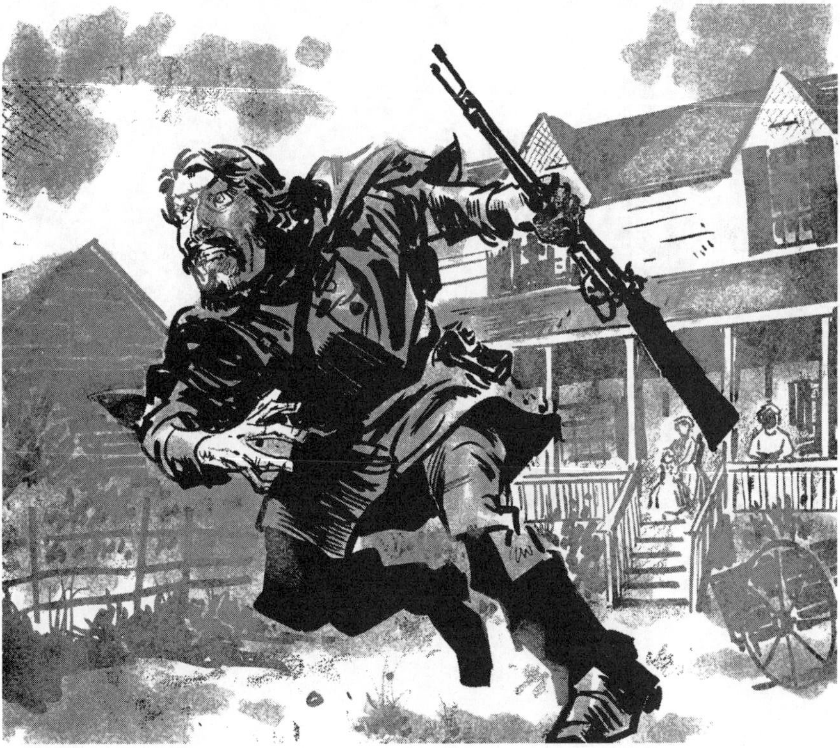

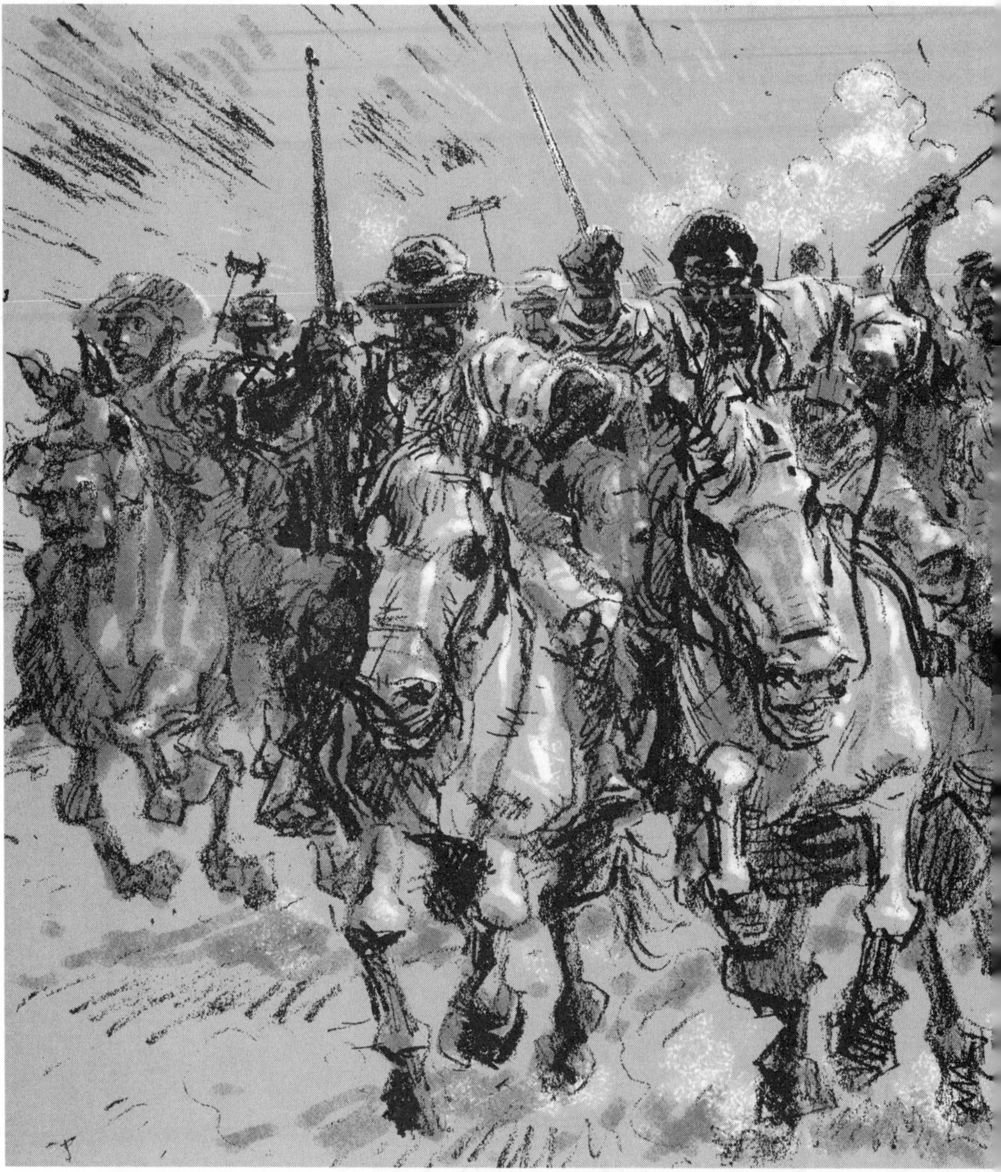

"*I* PROCEEDED TO MR. LEVI WALLER'S, TWO OR THREE MILES DISTANT. AS IT WAS MY OBJECT TO CARRY TERROR AND DEVASTATION WHEREVER WE WENT, I PLACED FIFTEEN OR TWENTY OF THE BEST ARMED AND MOST TO BE RELIED ON, IN FRONT, WHO GENERALLY APPROACHED THE HOUSES AS FAST AS THEIR HORSES COULD RUN; THIS WAS FOR TWO PURPOSES, TO PREVENT THEIR ESCAPE AND STRIKE TERROR TO THE INHABITANTS

"**H**AVING MURDERED MRS. WALLER AND TEN CHILDREN, WE STARTED FOR MR. WILLIAM WILLIAMS' - HAVING KILLED HIM AND TWO LITTLE BOYS THAT WERE THERE; WHILE ENGAGED IN THIS, MRS. WILLIAMS FLED AND GOT SOME DISTANCE FROM THE

HOUSE, BUT SHE WAS PURSUED, OVERTAKEN, AND COMPELLED TO GET UP BEHIND ONE OF THE COMPANY, WHO BROUGHT HER BACK, AND AFTER SHOWING HER THE MANGLED BODY OF HER LIFELESS HUSBAND, SHE WAS TOLD TO GET DOWN AND LAY BY HIS SIDE, WHERE SHE WAS SHOT DEAD.

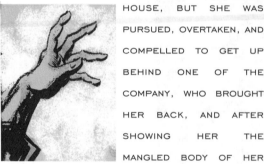

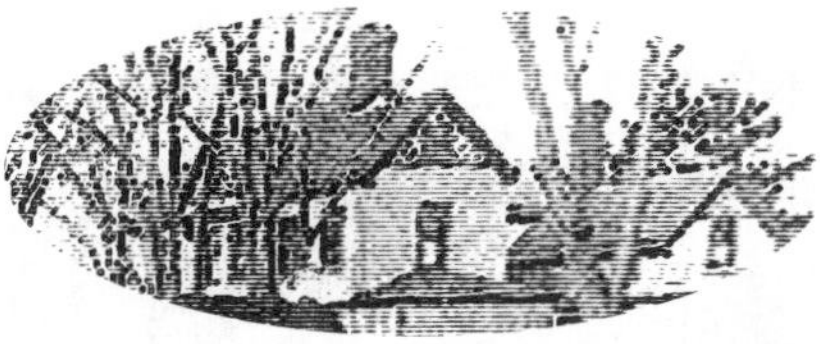

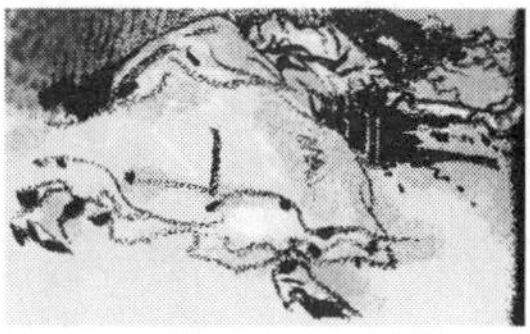

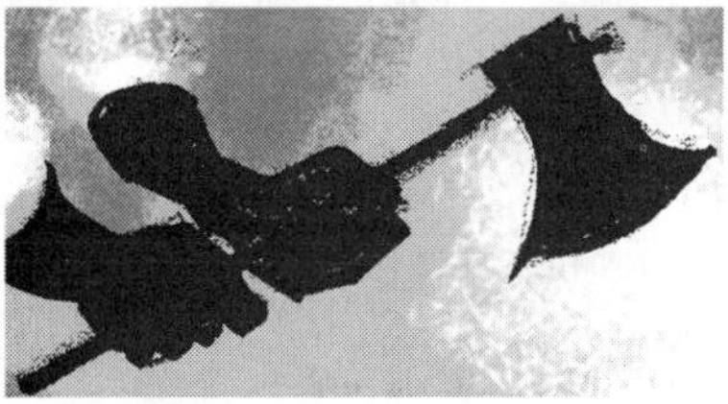

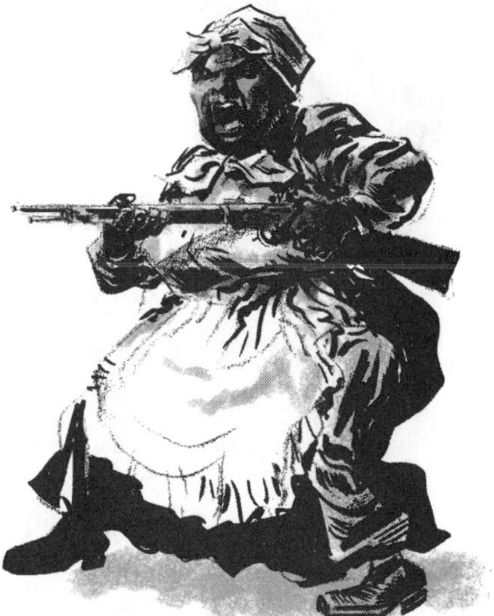

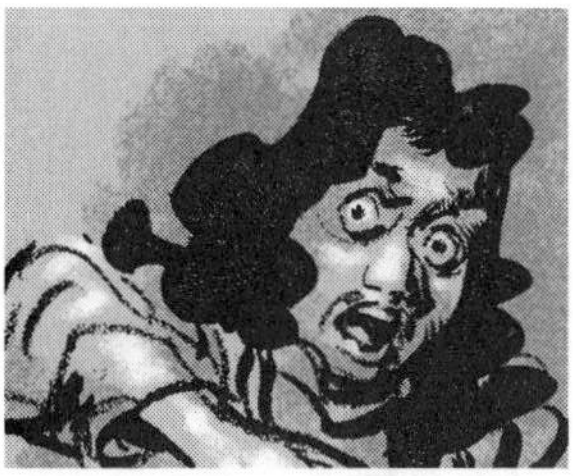

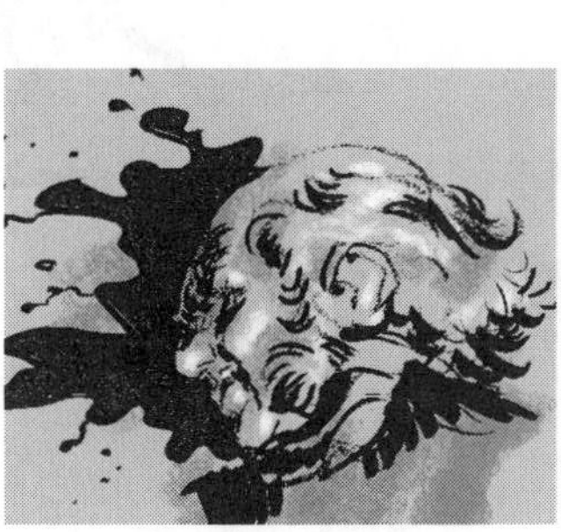

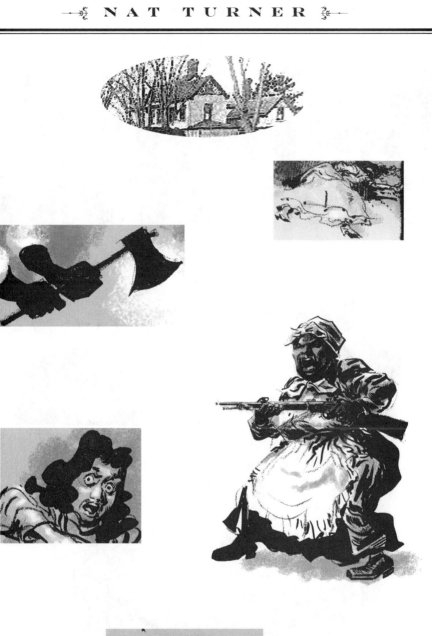

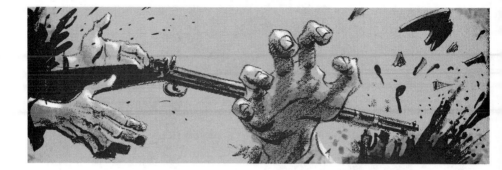

"*I* then started for Mr. Jacob Williams', where the family were murdered - Here we found a young man named Drury, who had come on business with Mr. Williams - he was

pursued, overtaken and shot. Mrs. Vaughan's was the next place we visited - and after murdering the family here, I determined on starting for Jerusalem

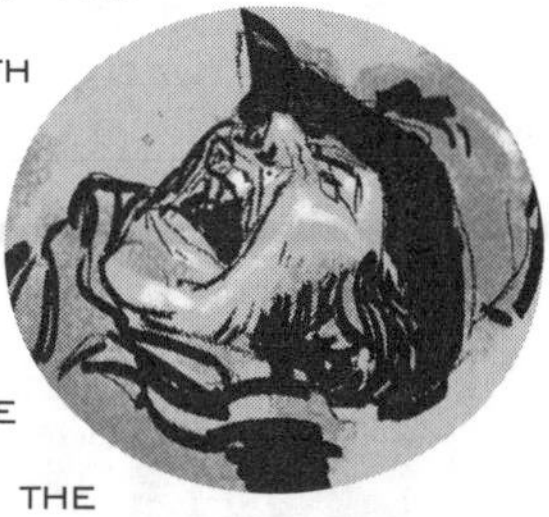

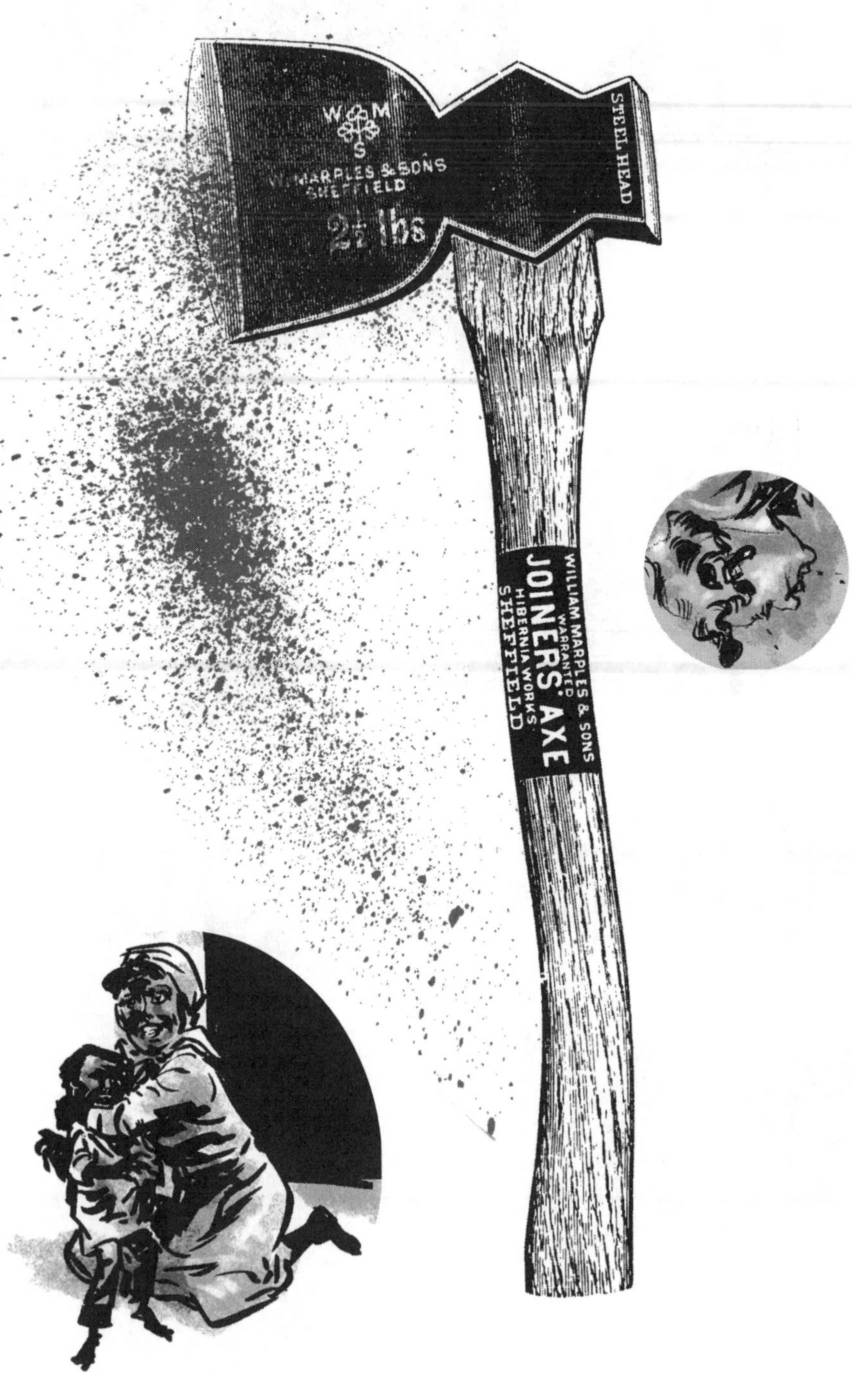
W M S
W. MARPLES & SONS
SHEFFIELD
2½ lbs
STEEL HEAD
WILLIAM MARPLES & SONS
WARRANTED
JOINERS' AXE
HIBERNIA WORKS
SHEFFIELD

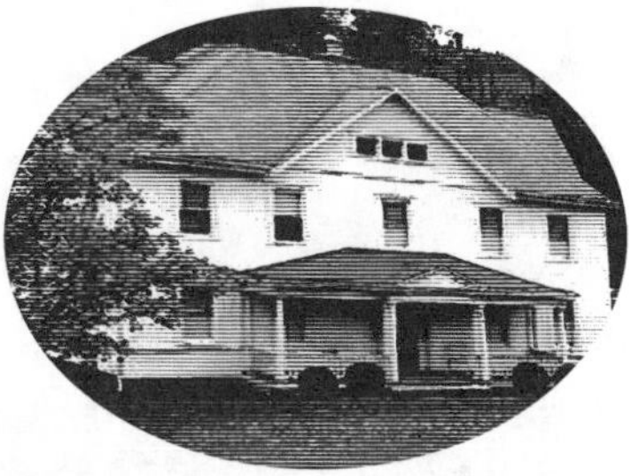

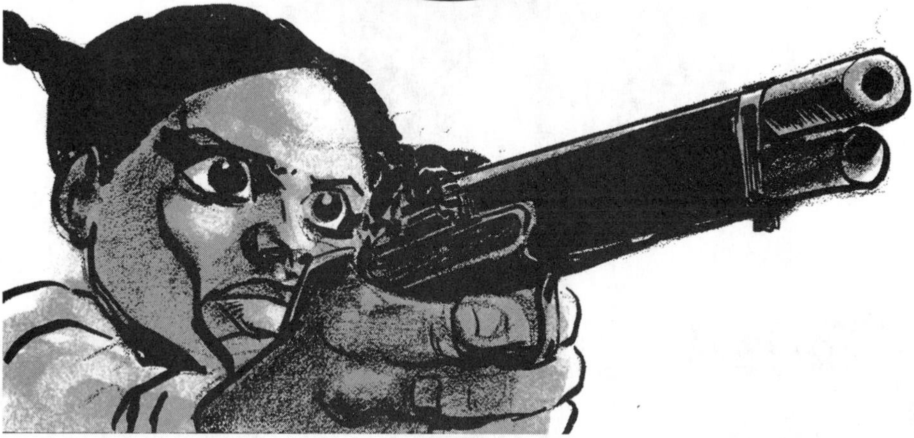

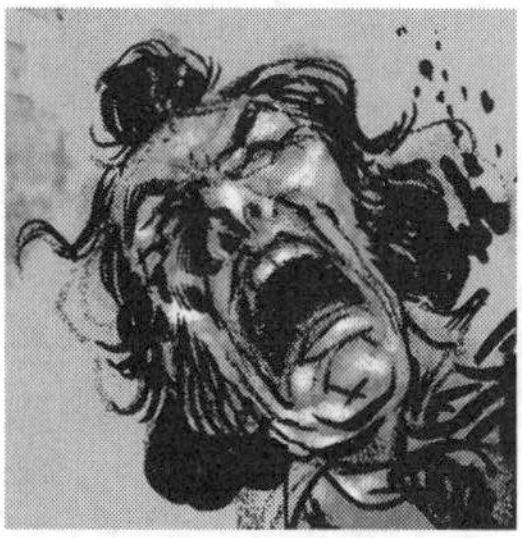

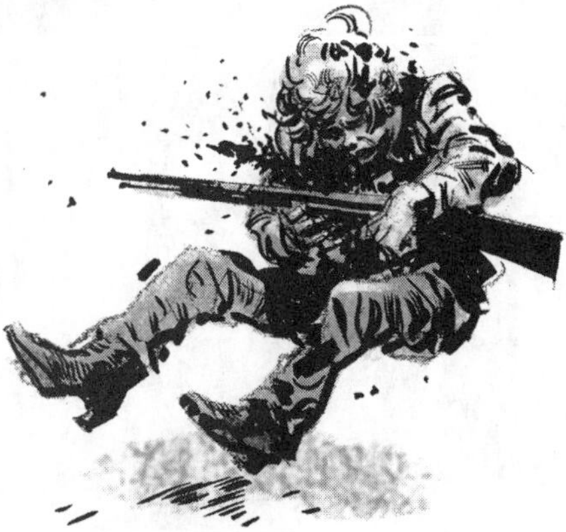

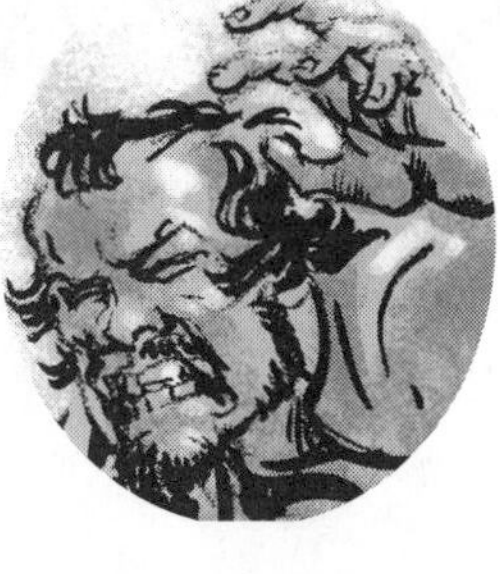

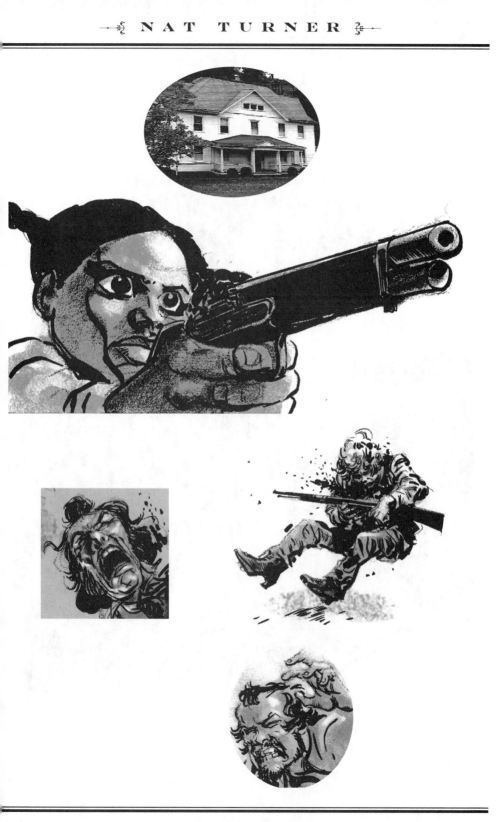

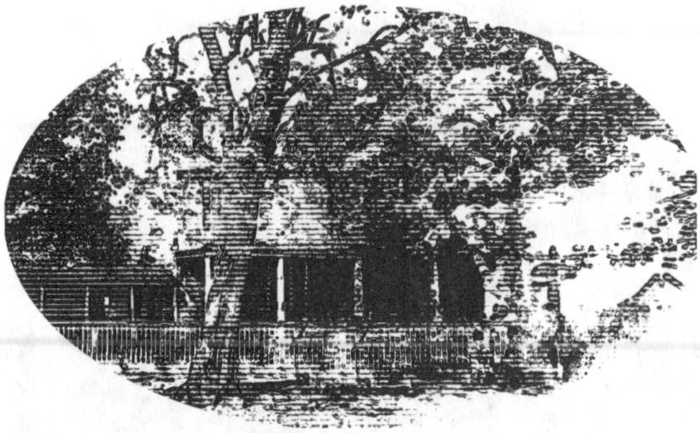

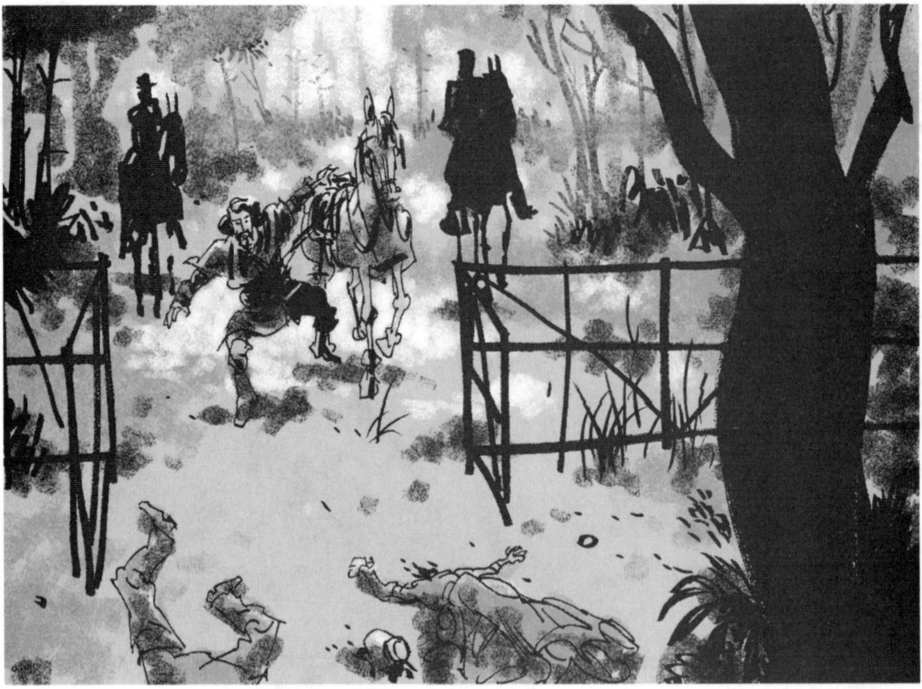

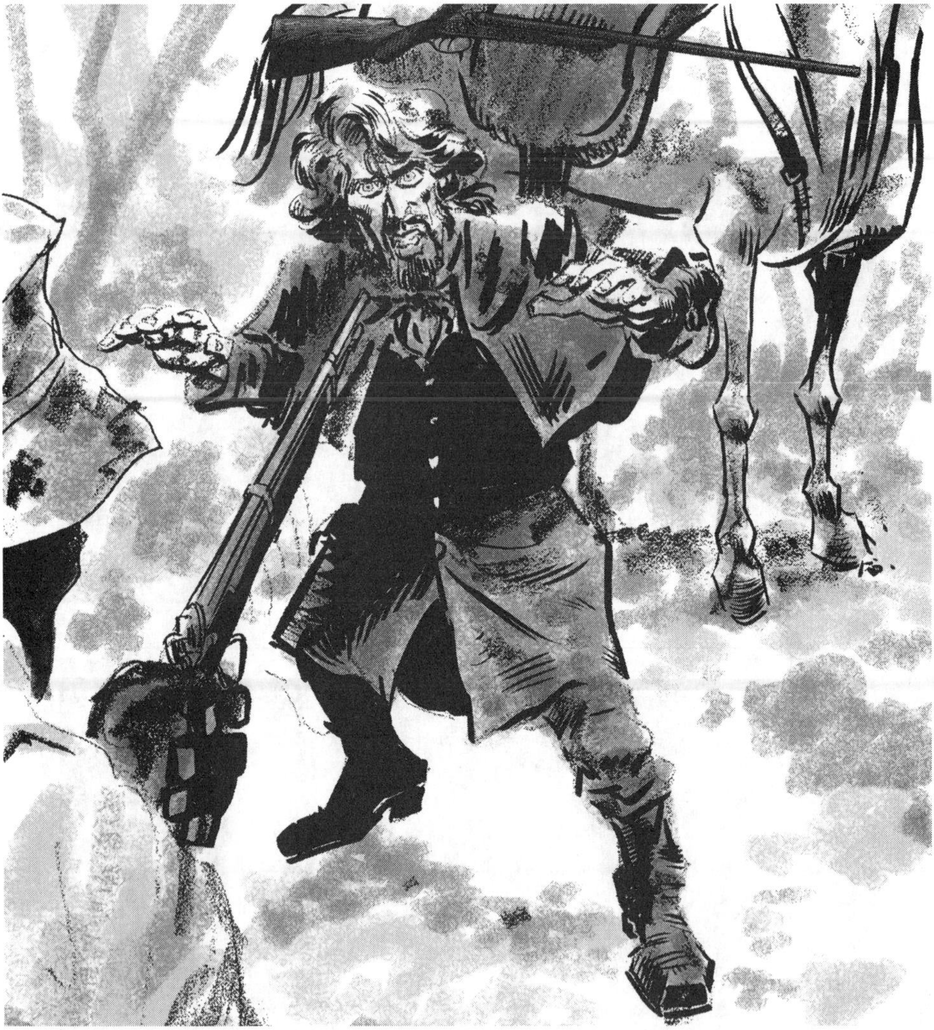

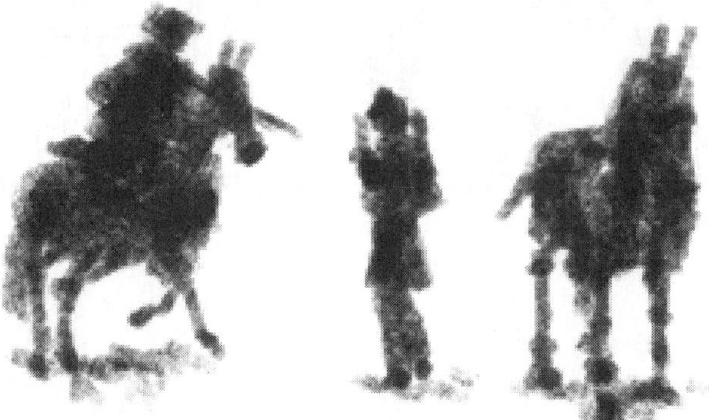

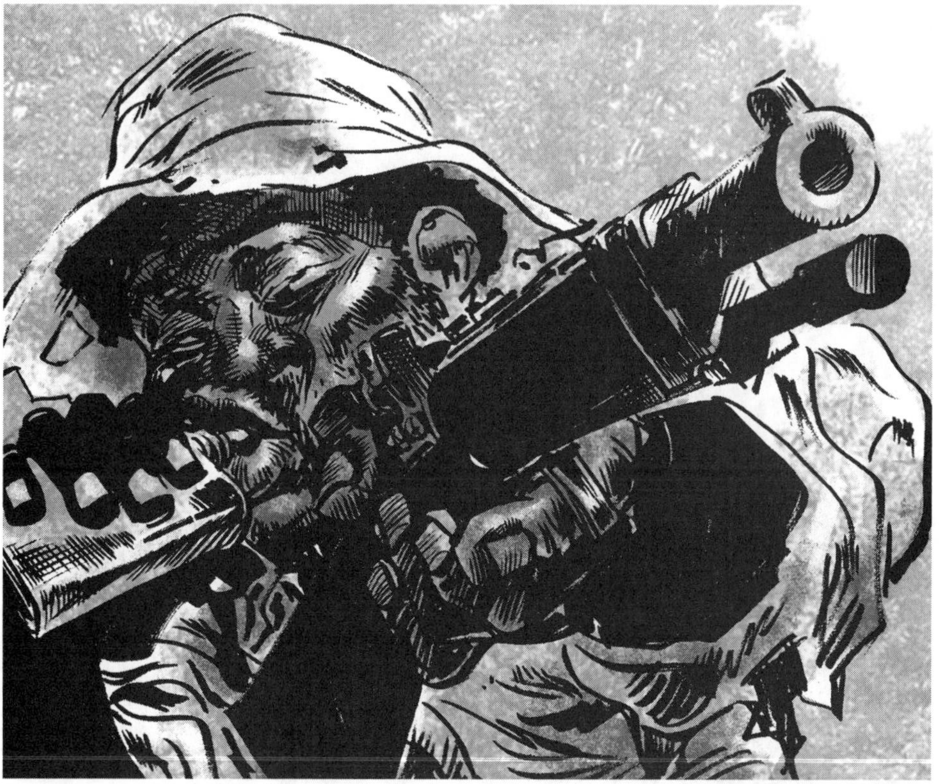

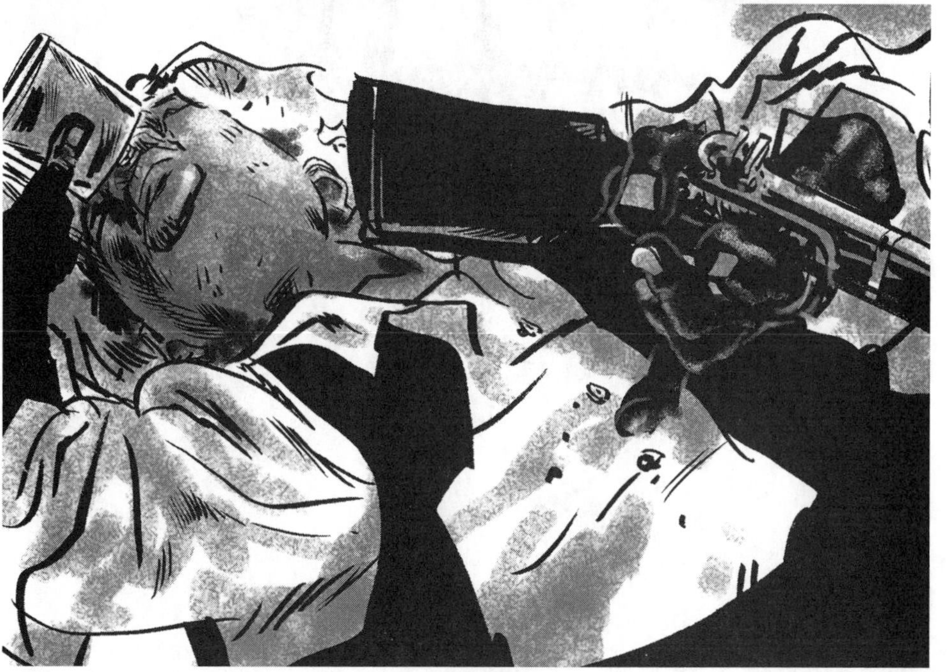

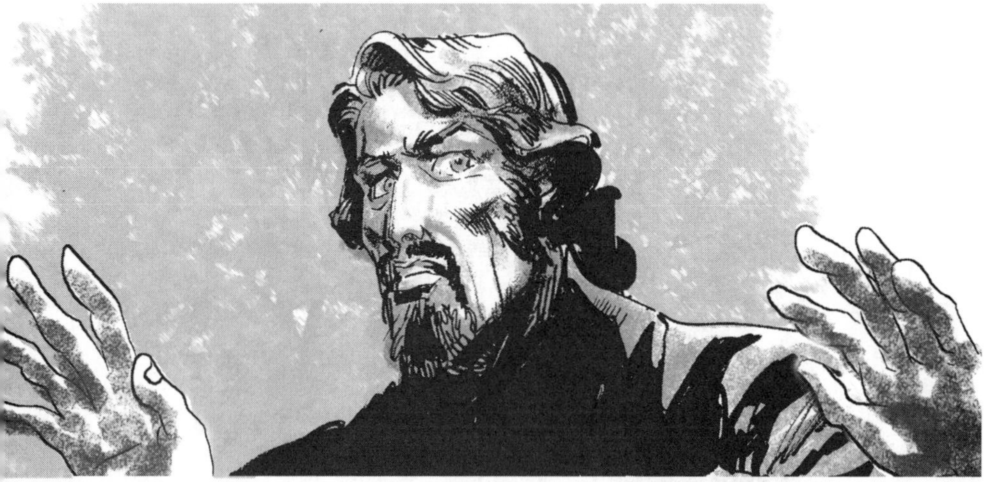

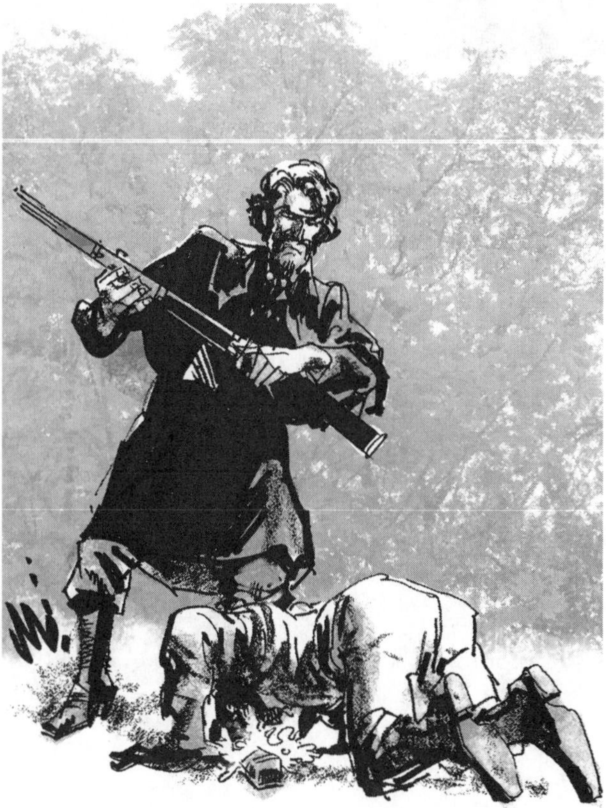

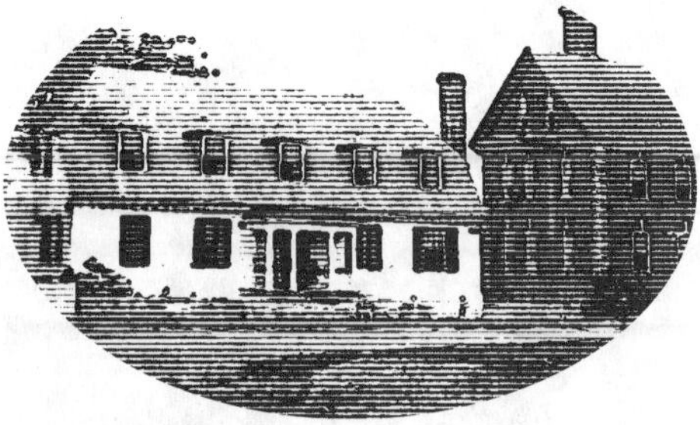

"OUR NUMBER AMOUNTED NOW TO FIFTY OR SIXTY, ALL MOUNTED AND ARMED WITH

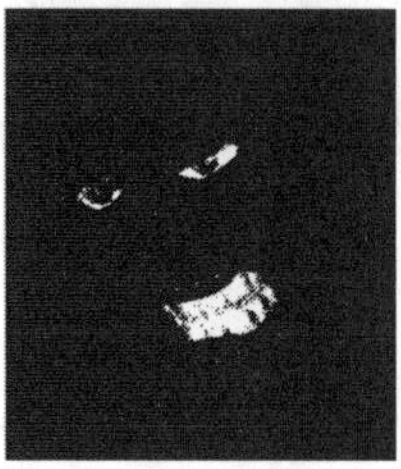

GUNS, AXES, SWORDS AND CLUBS- ON REACHING MR. JAMES W. PARKER'S GATE, IMMEDIATELY ON THE ROAD LEADING TO JERUSALEM, AND ABOUT THREE MILES DISTANT, IT WAS PROPOSED TO ME TO CALL THERE, BUT I OBJECTED, AS I KNEW HE WAS GONE TO JERUSALEM, AND MY OBJECT WAS TO REACH THERE AS SOON AS POSSIBLE; BUT SOME OF THE MEN HAVING RELATIONS AT MR. PARKER'S IT WAS AGREED THAT THEY MIGHT CALL AND GET HIS PEOPLE. I REMAINED AT THE GATE ON THE ROAD, WITH SEVEN OR EIGHT; THE OTHERS GOING ACROSS THE FIELD TO THE HOUSE, ABOUT HALF A MILE OFF.

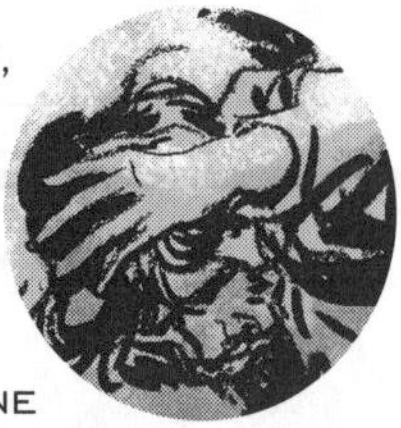

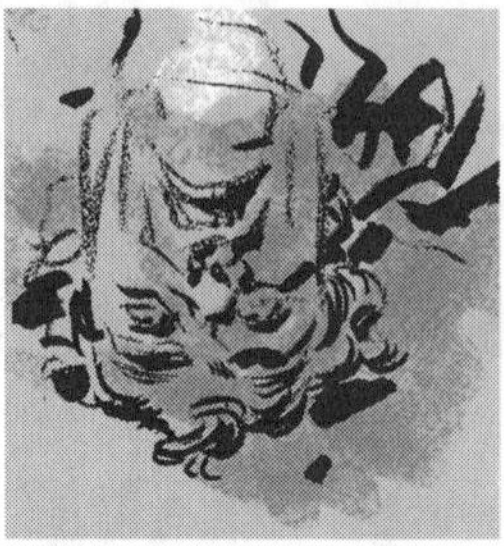

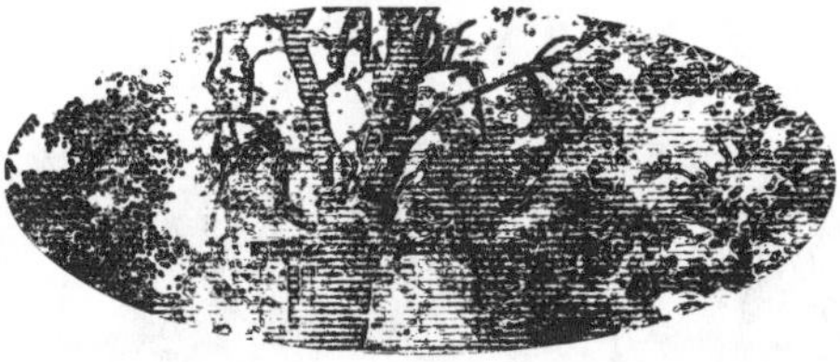

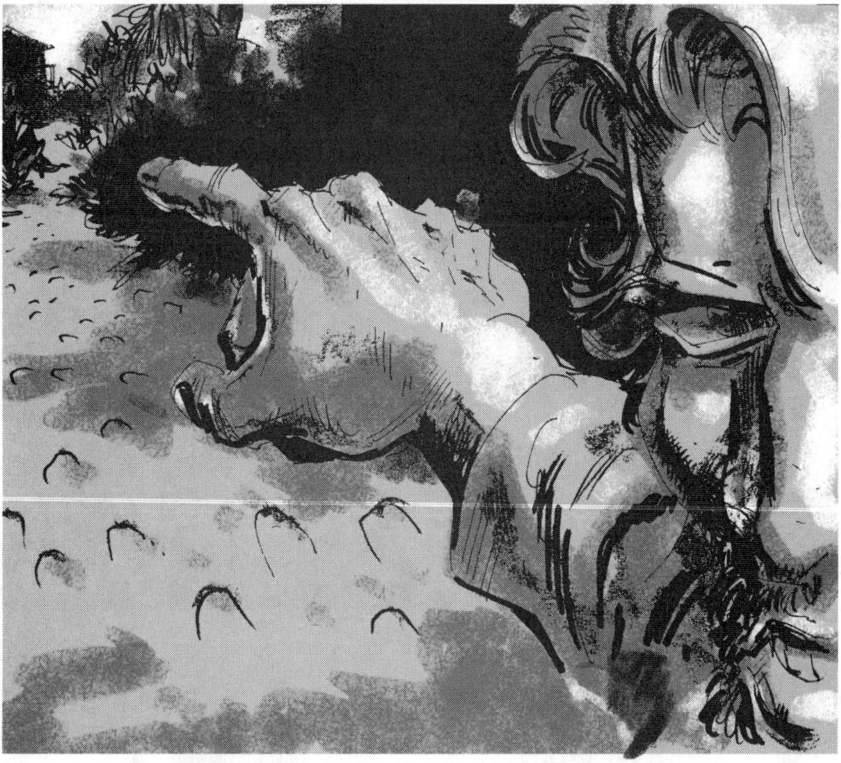

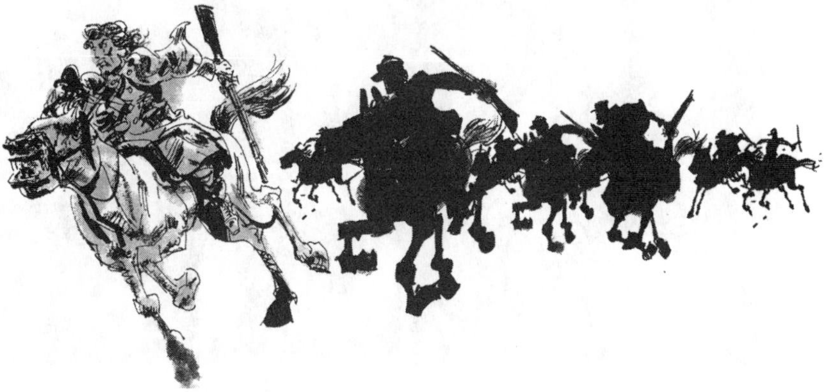

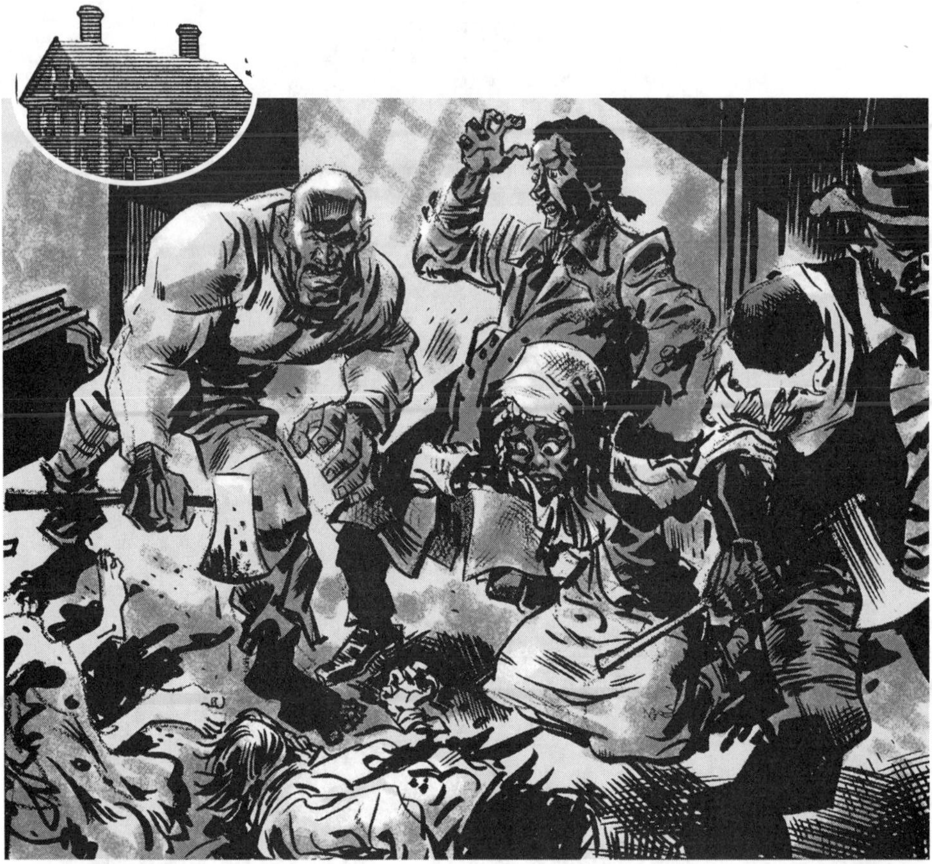

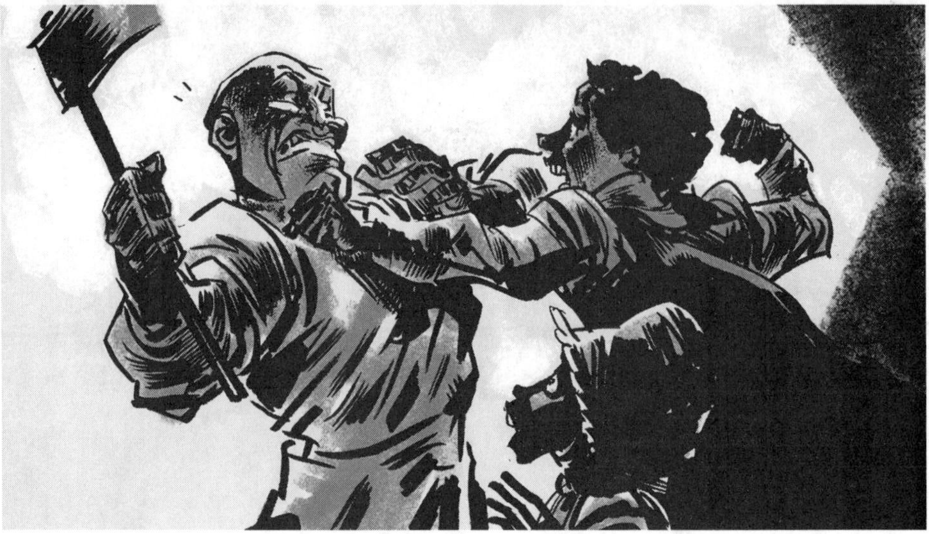

"*A*FTER WAITING SOME TIME FOR THEM, I BECAME
IMPATIENT ⁻ AND STARTED TO THE HOUSE FOR THEM⌒

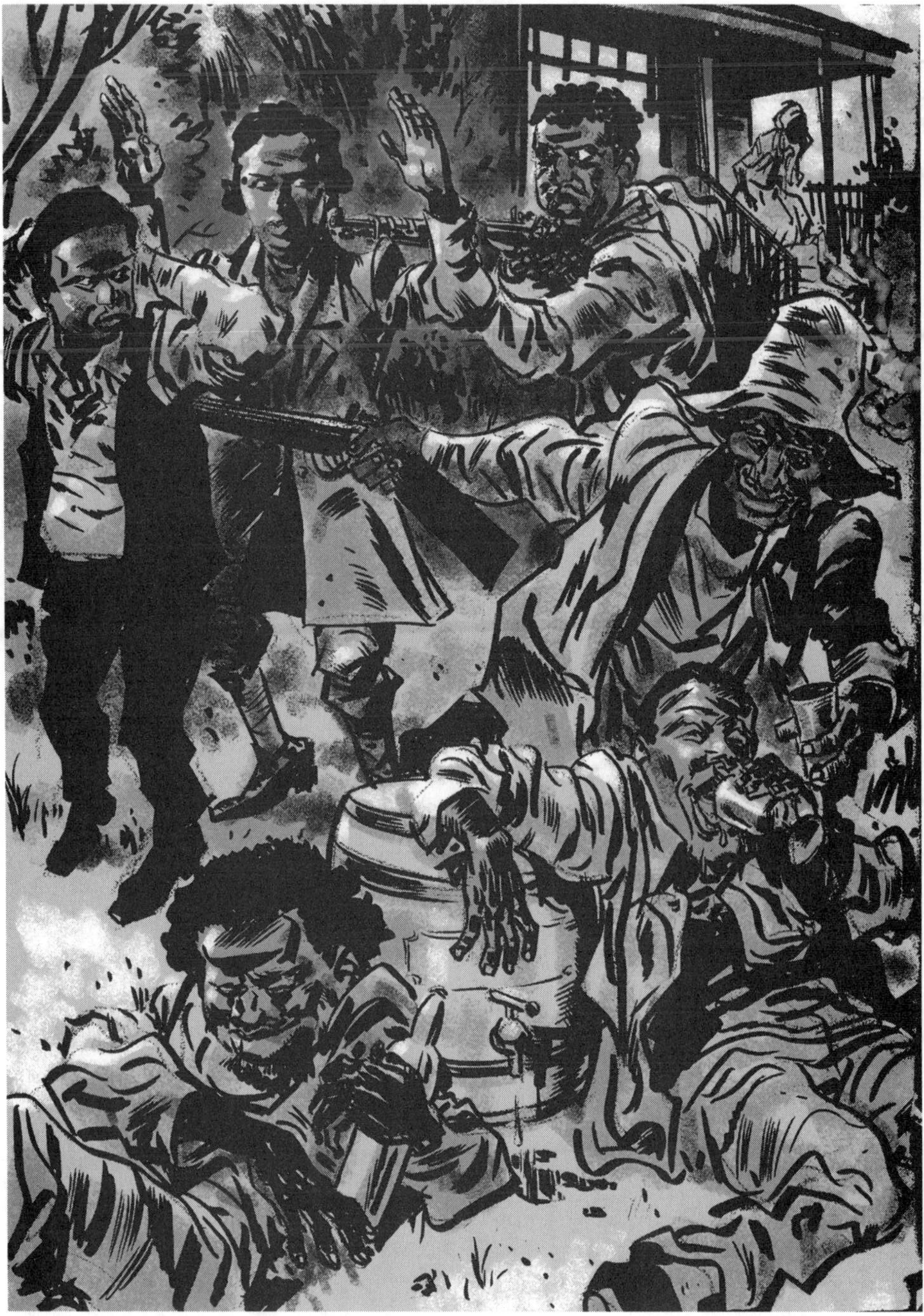

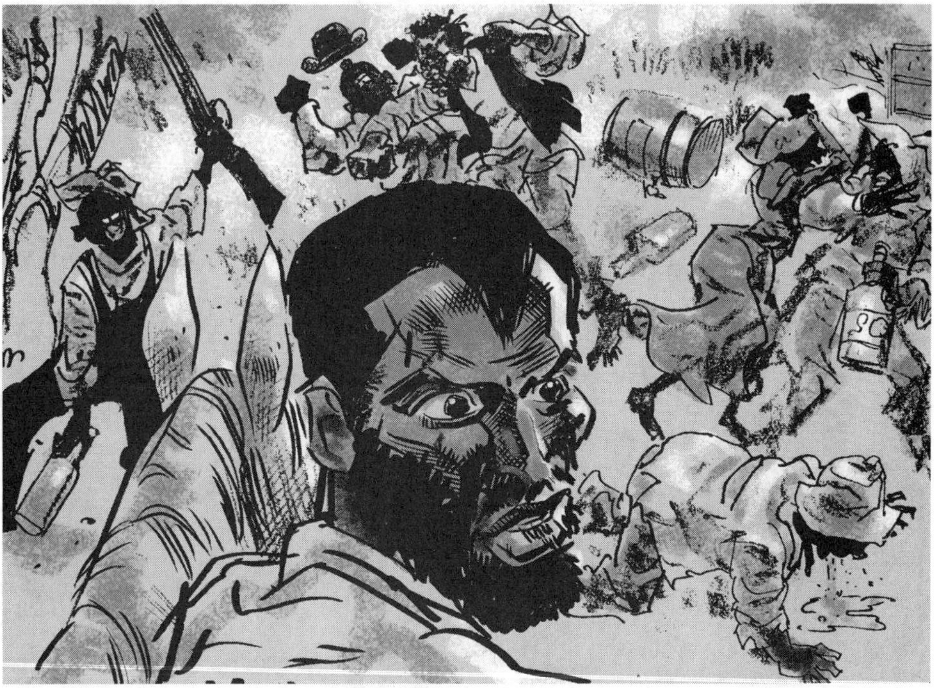

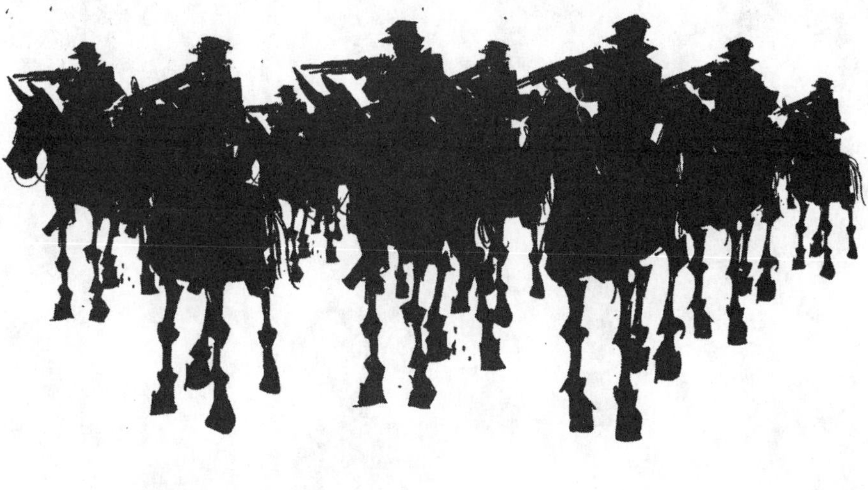

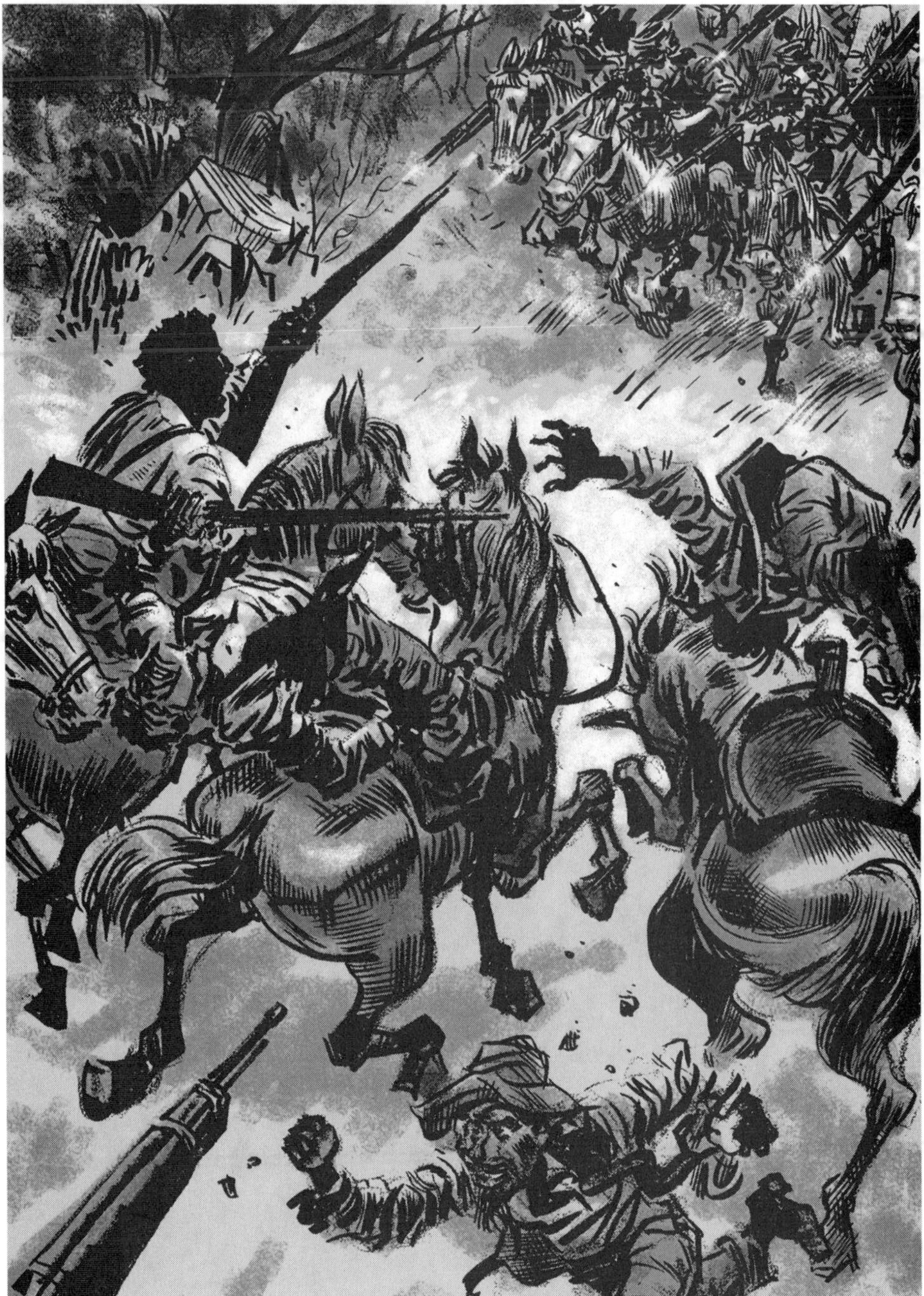

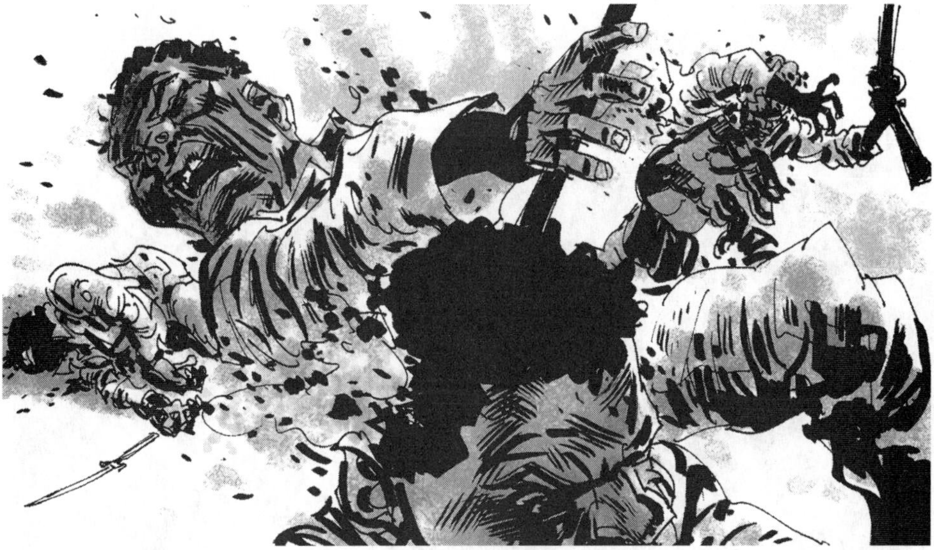

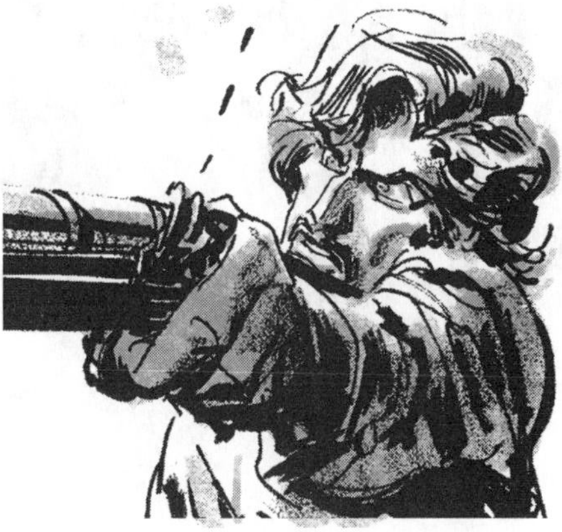

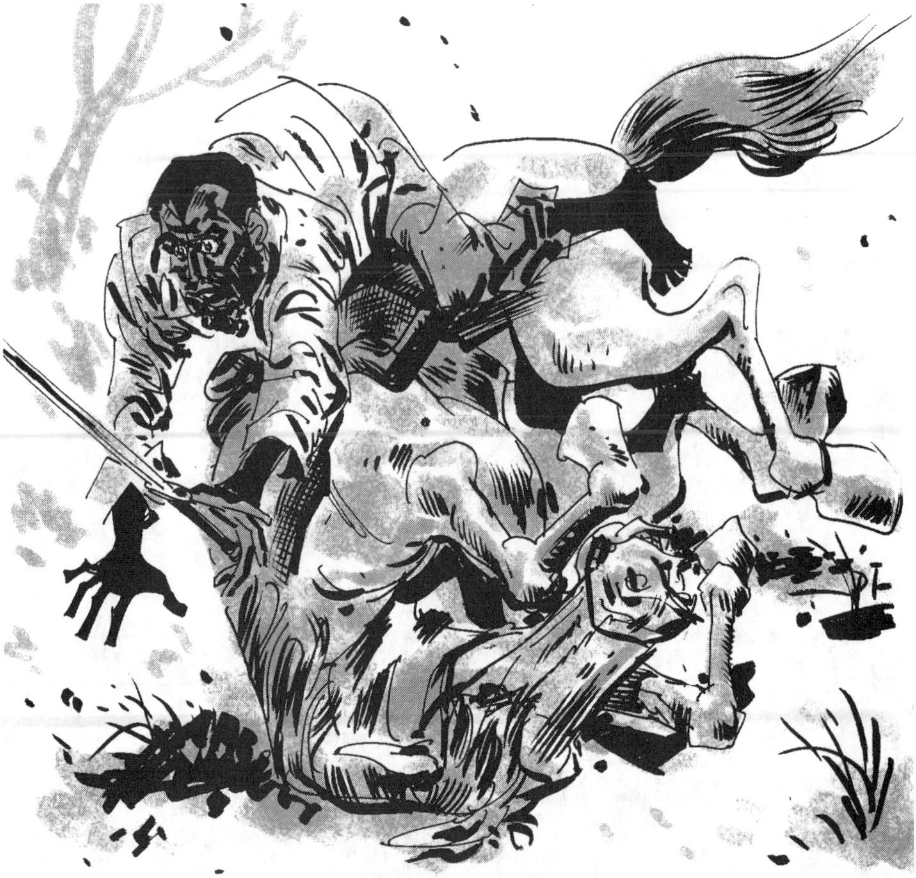

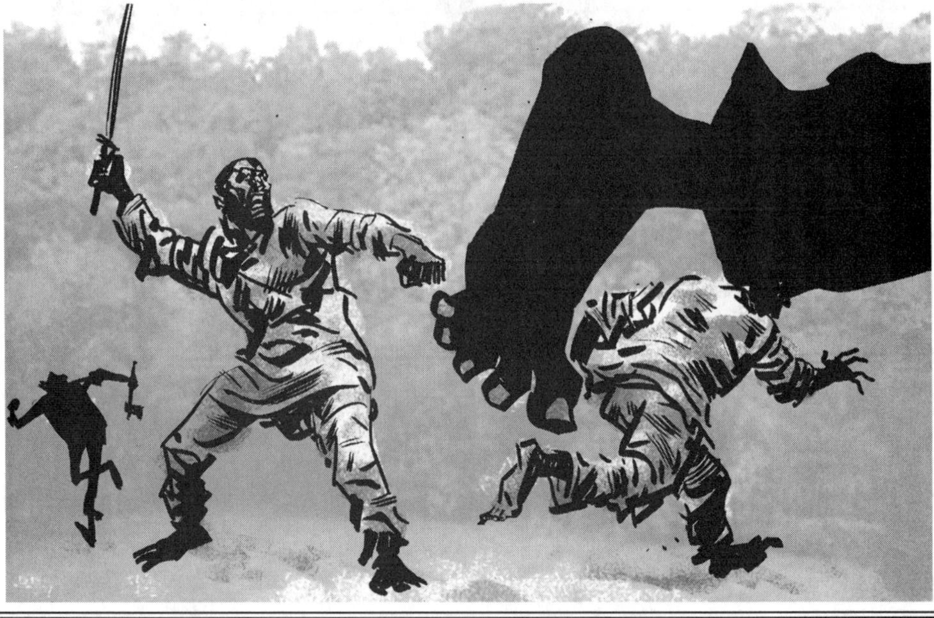

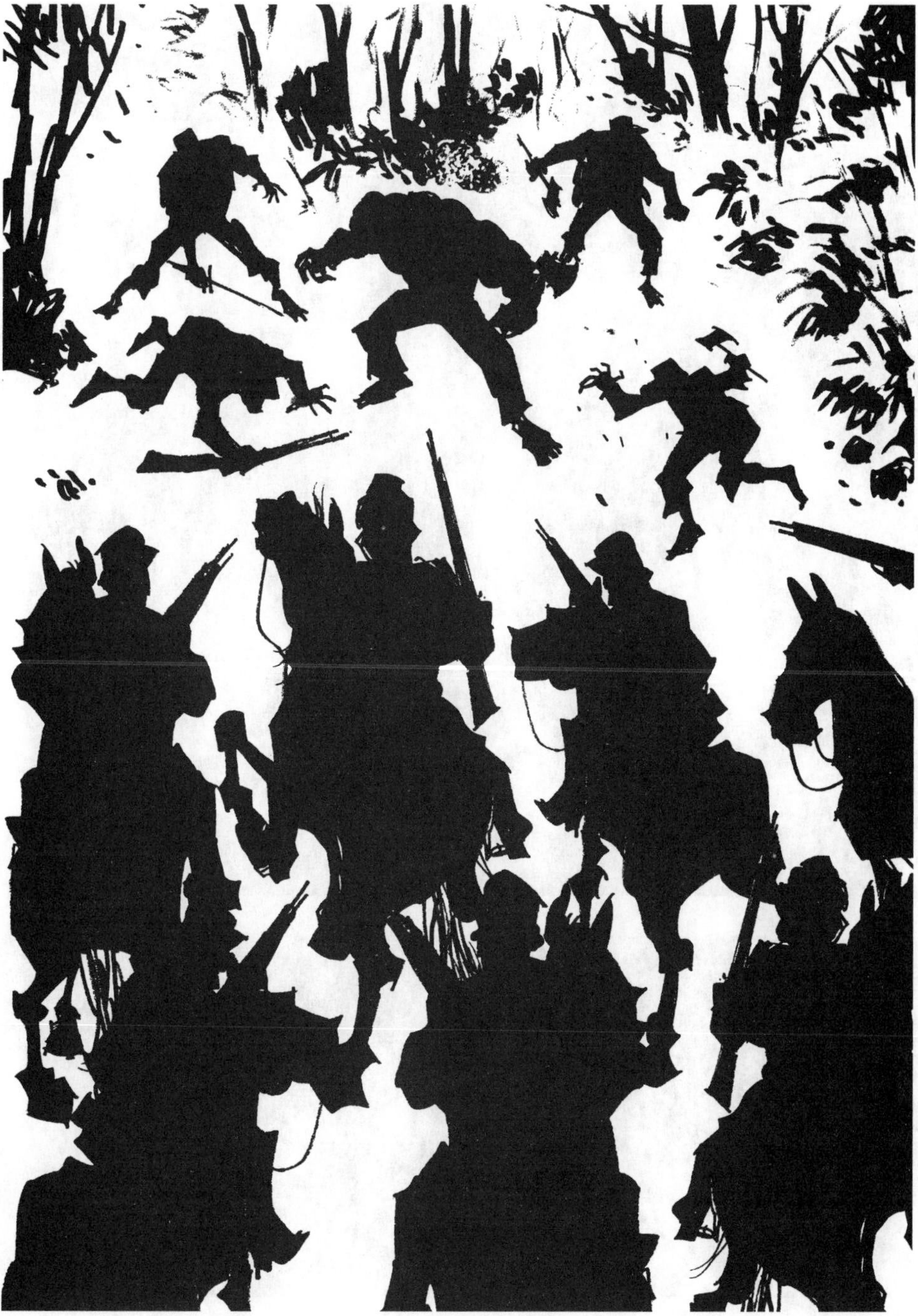

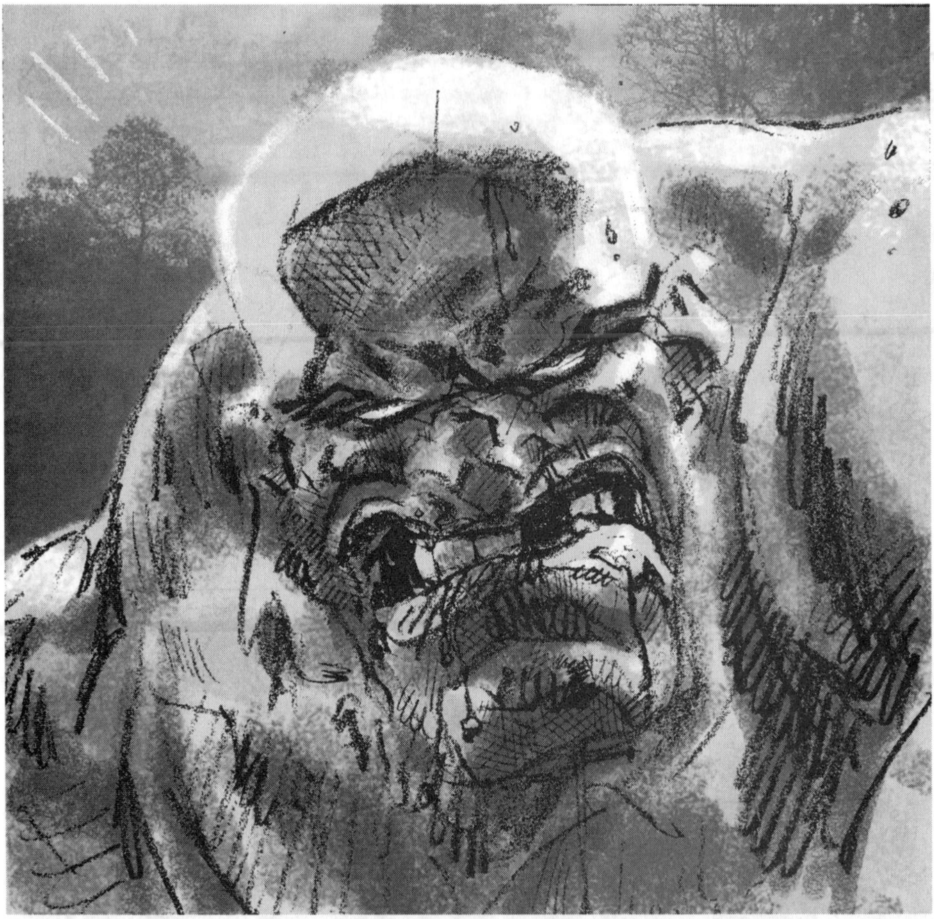

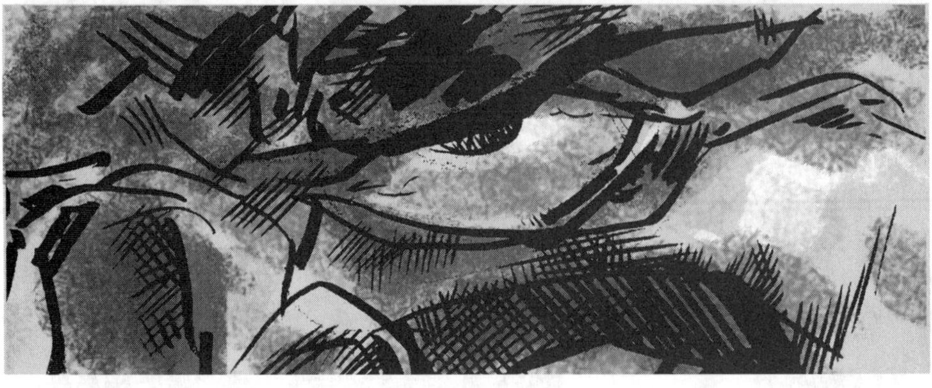

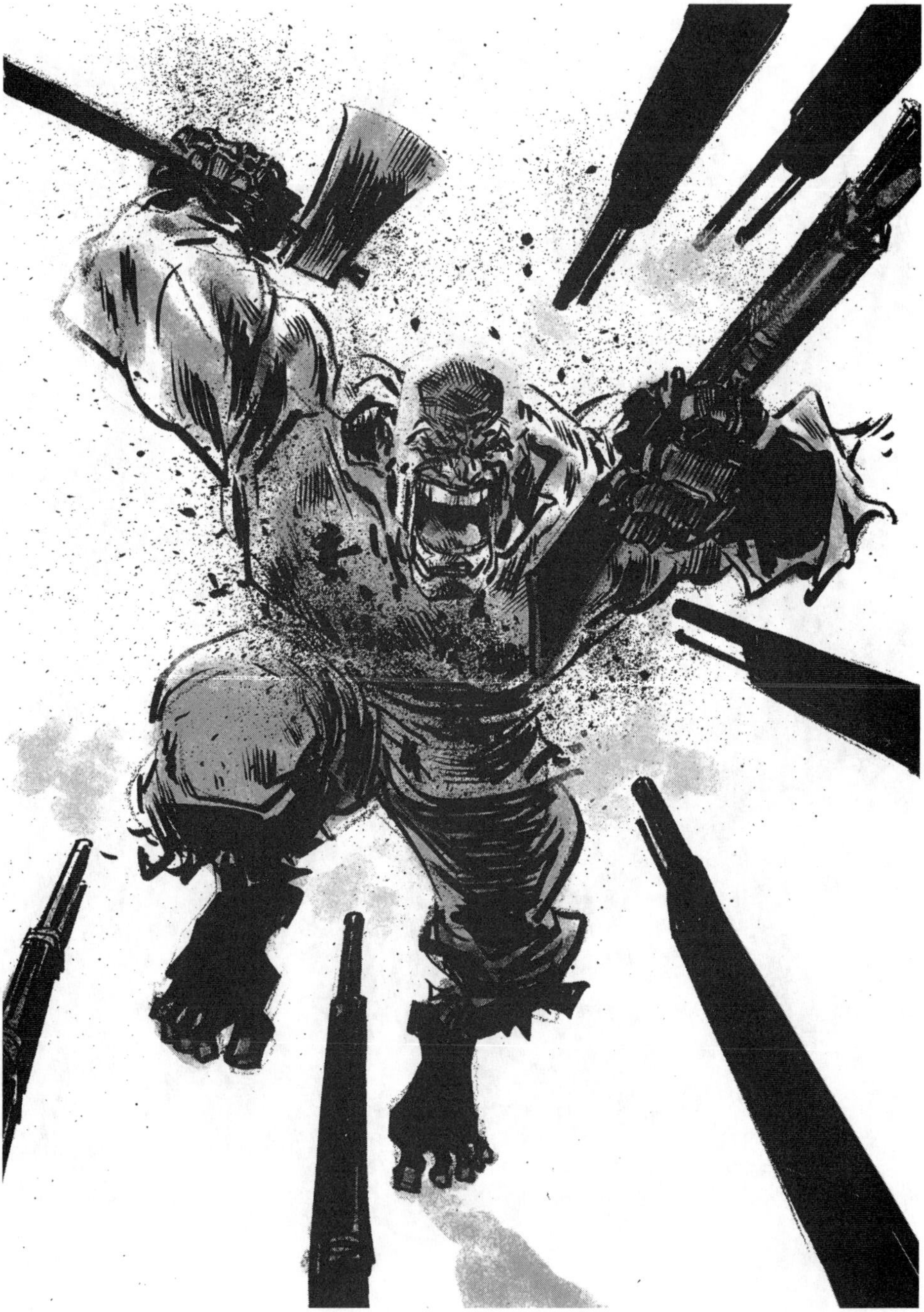

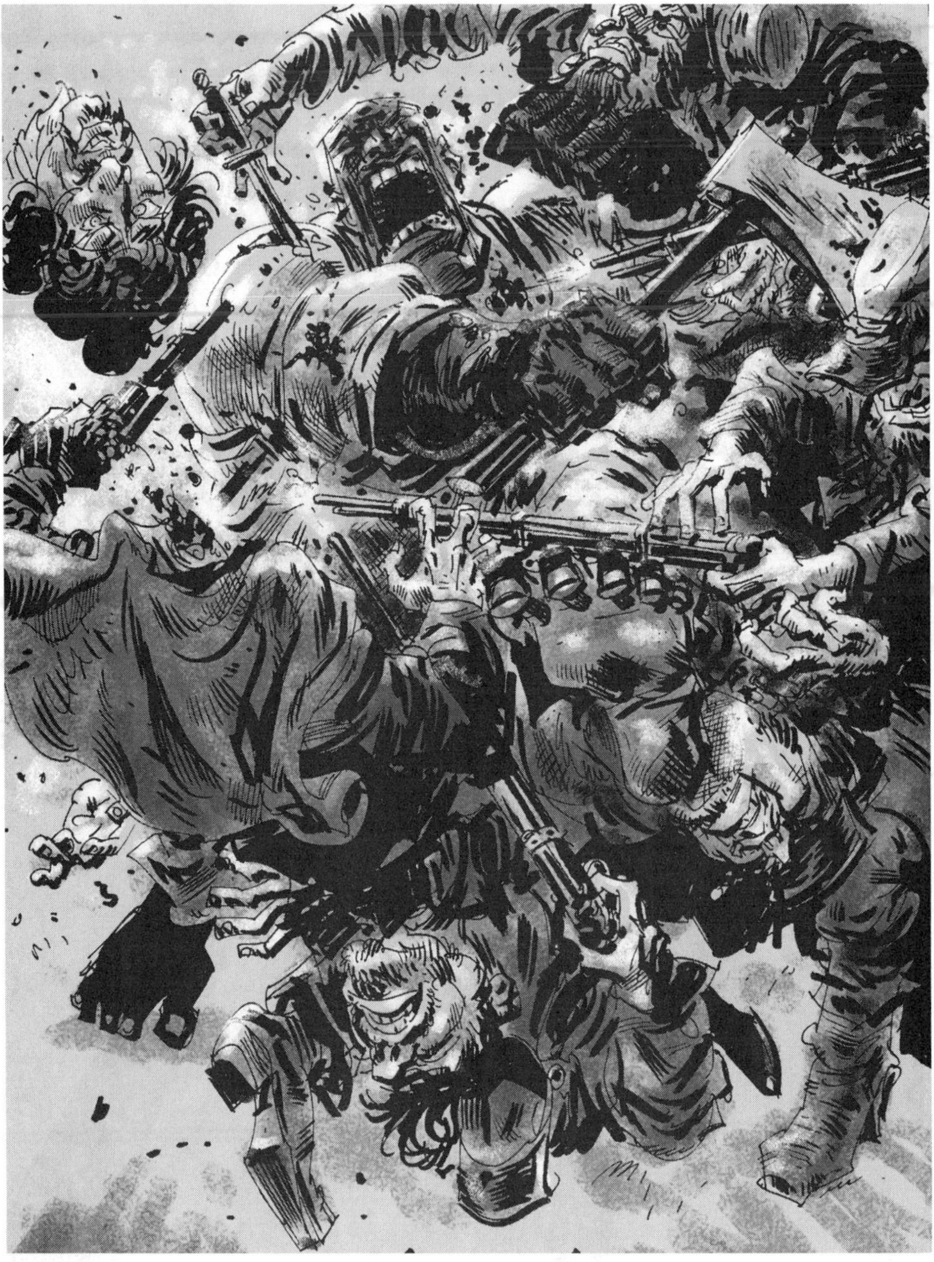

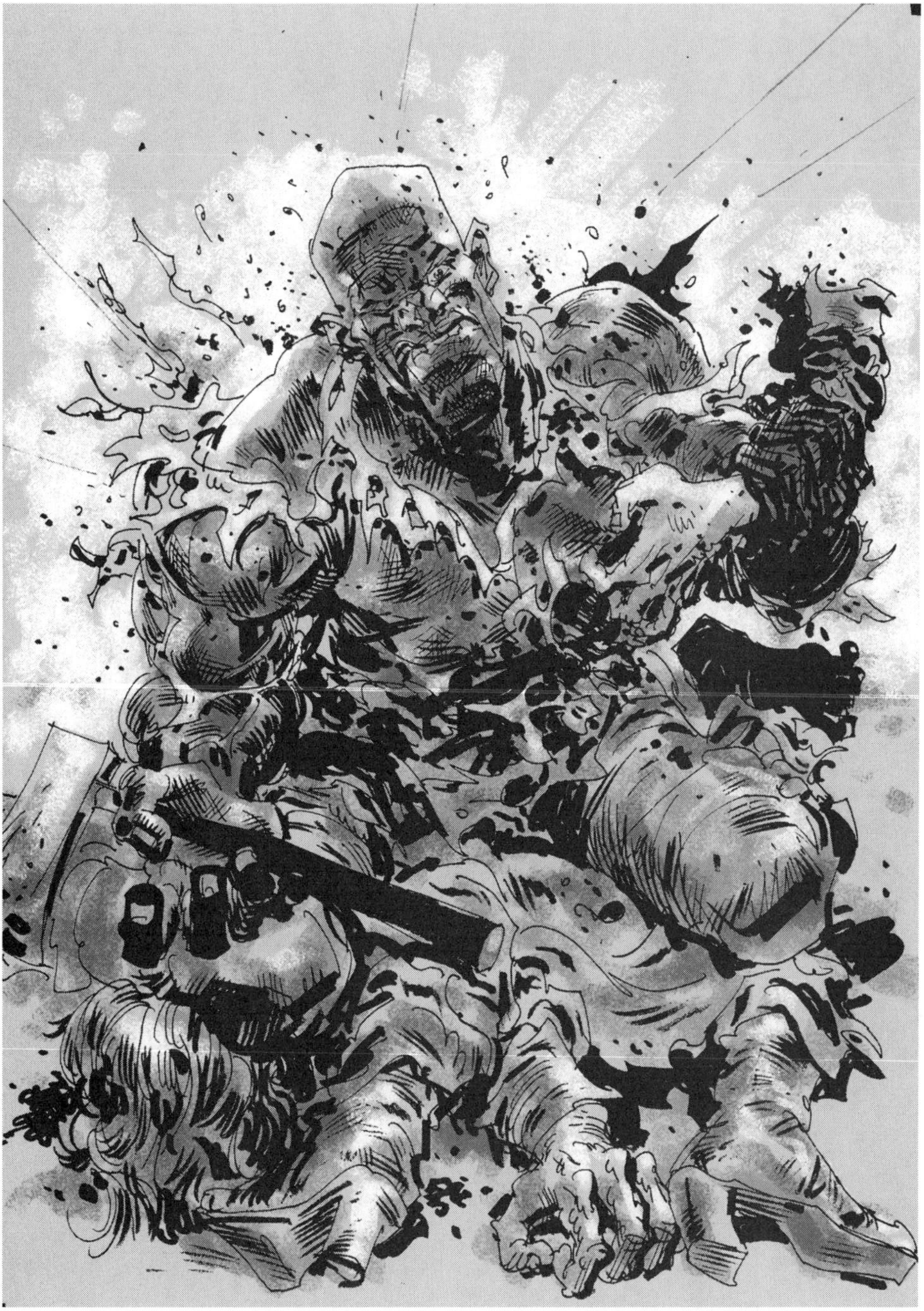

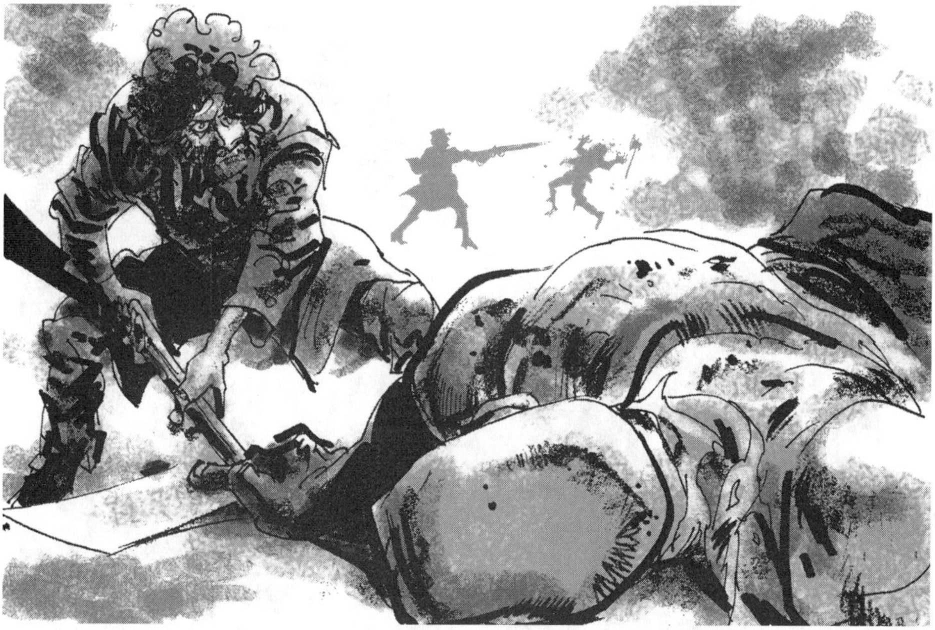

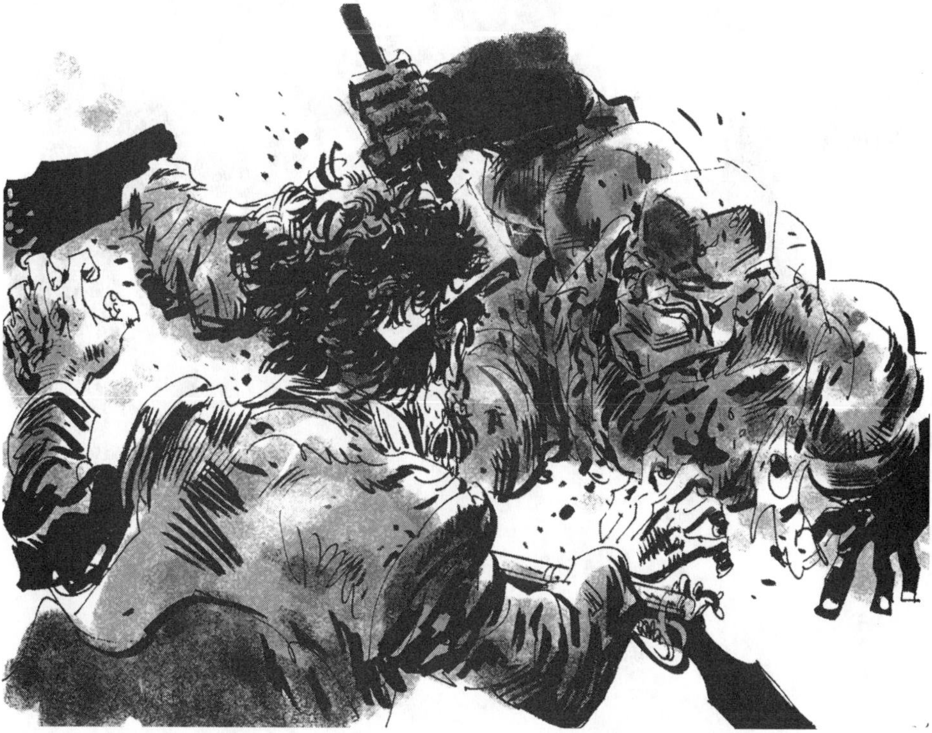

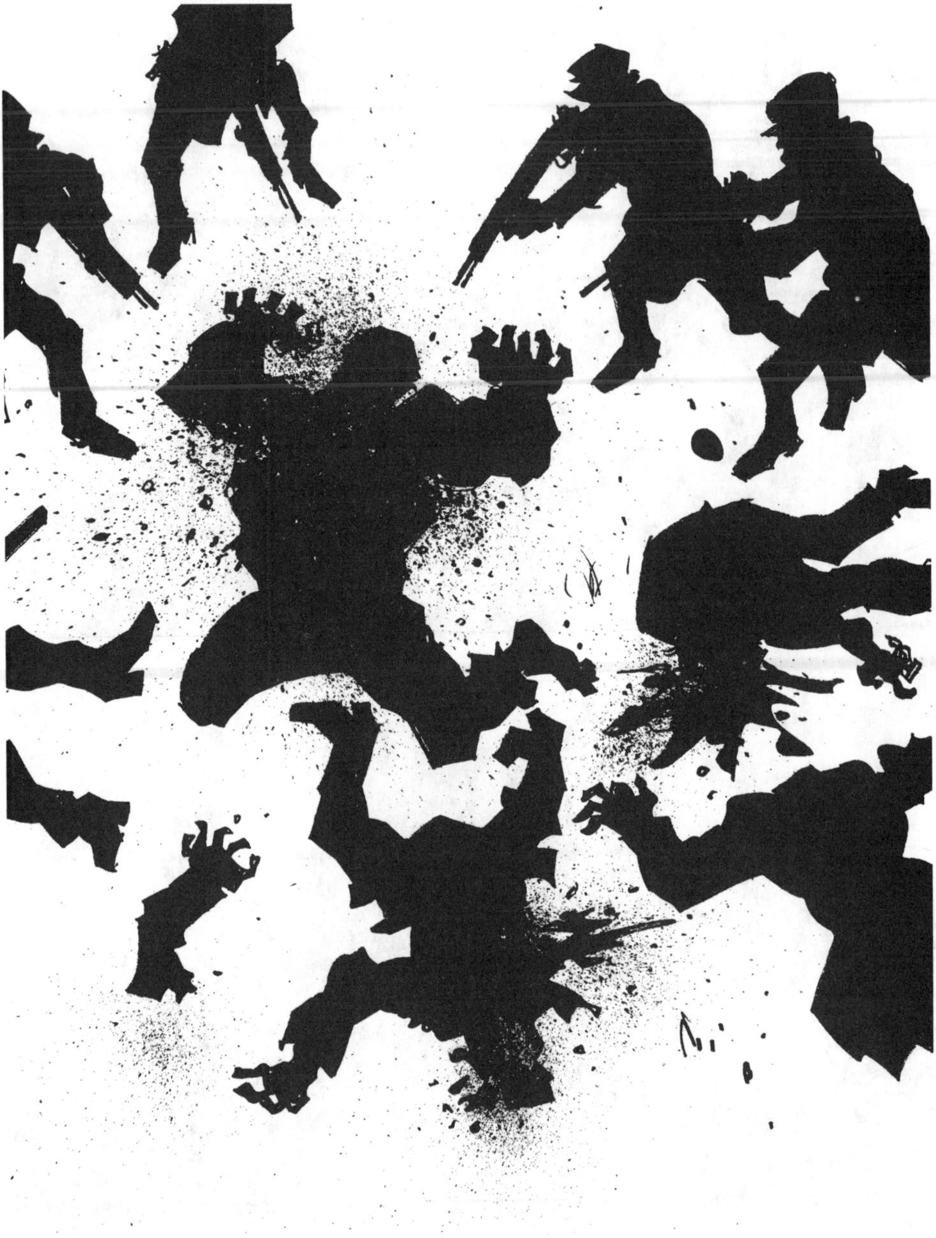

A list of persons murdered in the Insurrection, on the 21st and 22d of August, 1831.

* Joseph Travers and wife and three children,

* Mrs. Elizabeth Turner,

* Hartwell Prebles,

* Sarah Newsome,

* Mrs. P. Reese and son William,

* Trajan Doyle,

* Henry Bryant and wife and child, and wife's mother,

* Mrs. Catherine Whitehead, son Richard and four daughters and grandchild,

* Salathiel Francis,

* Nathaniel Francis' overseer and two children,

* John T. Barrow,

* George Vaughan,

* Mrs. Levi Waller and ten children,

* William Williams, wife and two boys,

* Mrs. Caswell Worrell and child,

* Mrs. Rebecca Vaughan,

* Ann Eliza Vaughan, and son Arthur,

* Mrs. John K. Williams and child,

* Mrs. Jacob Williams and three children,

* and Edwin Drury

-amounting to fifty-five.

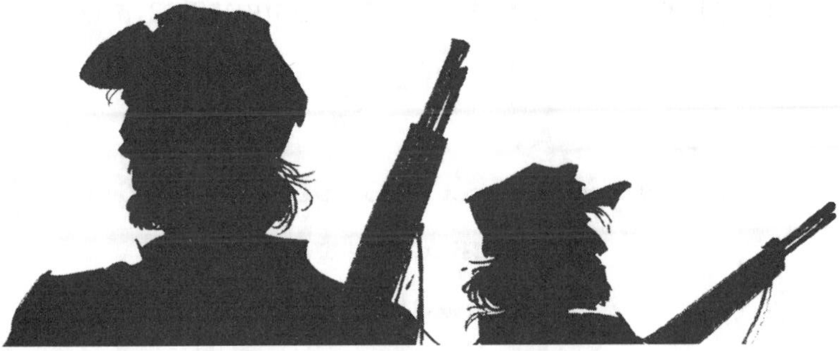

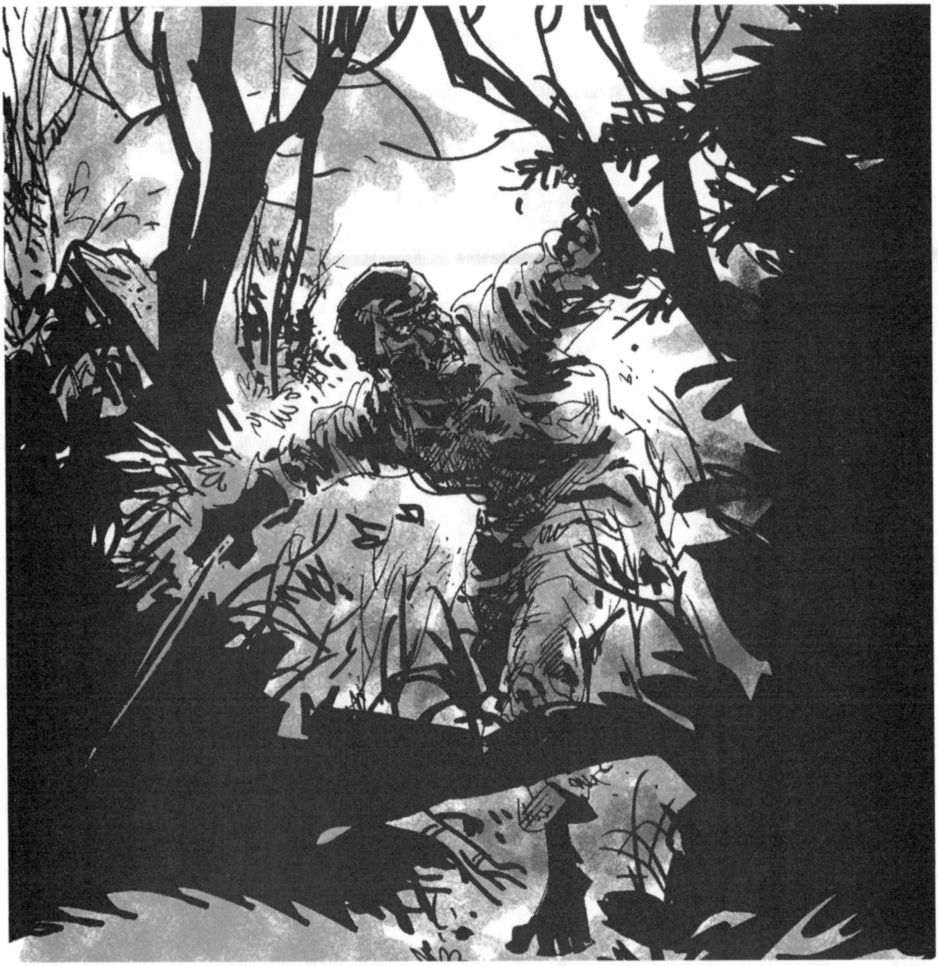

"*P*URSUING OUR COURSE BACK, AND COMING IN SIGHT OF CAPTAIN HARRIS'S, WHERE WE HAD BEEN THE DAY BEFORE, WE DISCOVERED A PARTY OF WHITE MEN AT THE HOUSE, ON WHICH ALL DESERTED ME BUT TWO, (JACOB AND NAT,) WE CONCEALED OURSELVES IN THE WOODS UNTIL NEAR NIGHT, WHEN I SENT THEM IN SEARCH OF HENRY, SAM, NELSON AND HARK, AND DIRECTED THEM TO RALLY ALL THEY COULD, AT THE PLACE WE HAD HAD OUR DINNER THE SUNDAY BEFORE, WHERE THEY WOULD FIND ME, AND I ACCORDINGLY RETURNED THERE AS SOON AS IT WAS DARK, AND REMAINED UNTIL WEDNESDAY EVENING, WHEN DISCOVERING WHITE MEN RIDING AROUND THE PLACE AS THOUGH THEY WERE LOOKING FOR SOME ONE, AND NONE OF MY MEN JOINING ME, I CONCLUDED JACOB AND NAT HAD BEEN TAKEN, AND COMPELLED TO BETRAY ME. ON THIS I GAVE UP ALL HOPE FOR THE PRESENT;

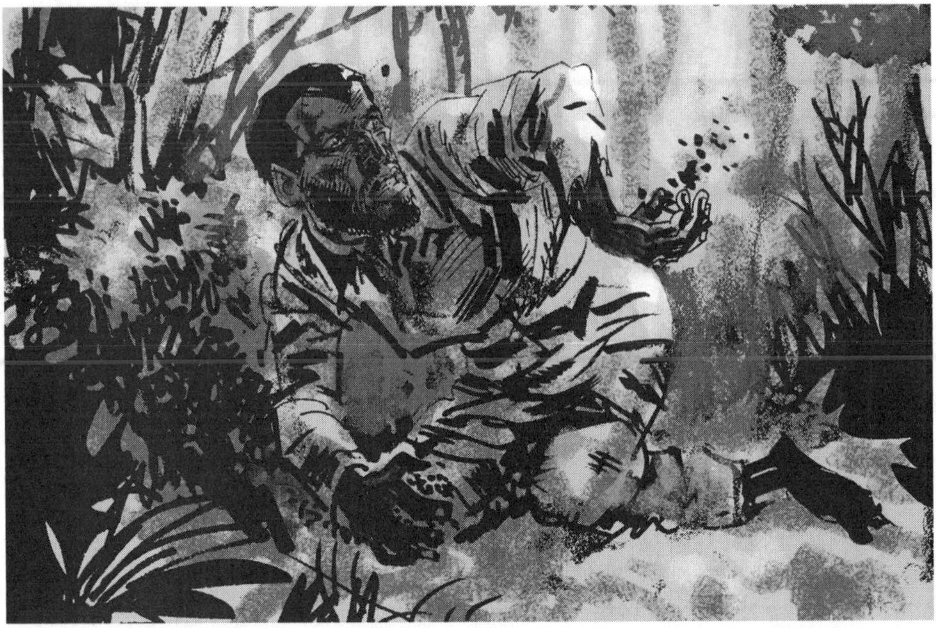

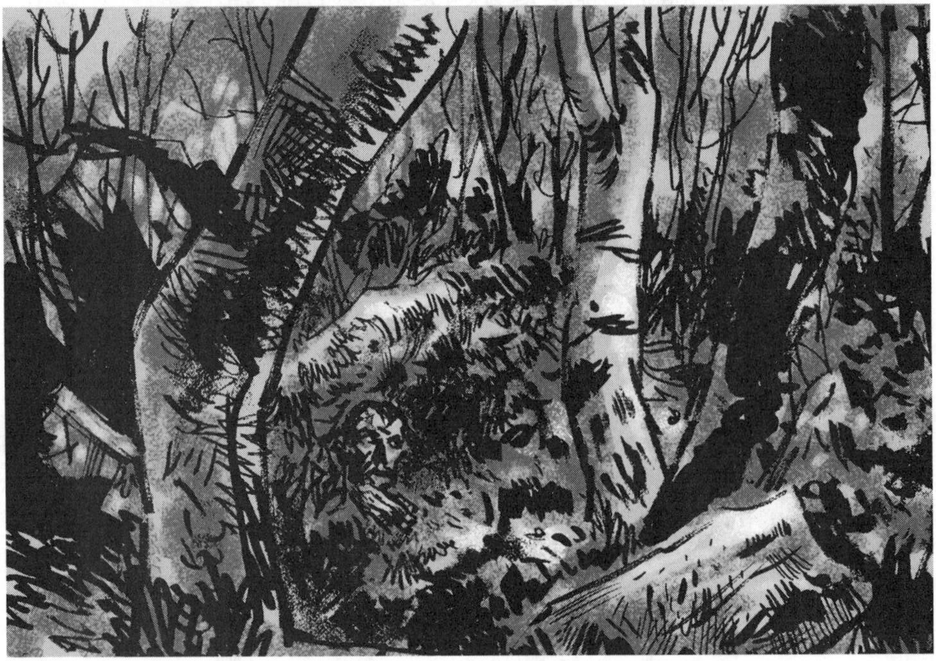

"*I* CONCEALED MYSELF FOR SIX WEEKS, NEVER LEAVING MY HIDING PLACE BUT FOR A FEW MINUTES IN THE DEAD OF NIGHT TO GET WATER, WHICH WAS VERY NEAR; THINKING BY THIS TIME I COULD VENTURE OUT, I BEGAN TO GO ABOUT IN THE NIGHT AND EAVES DROP THE HOUSES IN THE NEIGHBORHOOD; PURSUING THIS COURSE FOR ABOUT A FORTNIGHT AND GATHERING LITTLE OR NO INTELLIGENCE, AFRAID OF SPEAKING TO ANY HUMAN BEING, AND RETURNING EVERY MORNING TO MY CAVE BEFORE THE DAWN OF DAY.

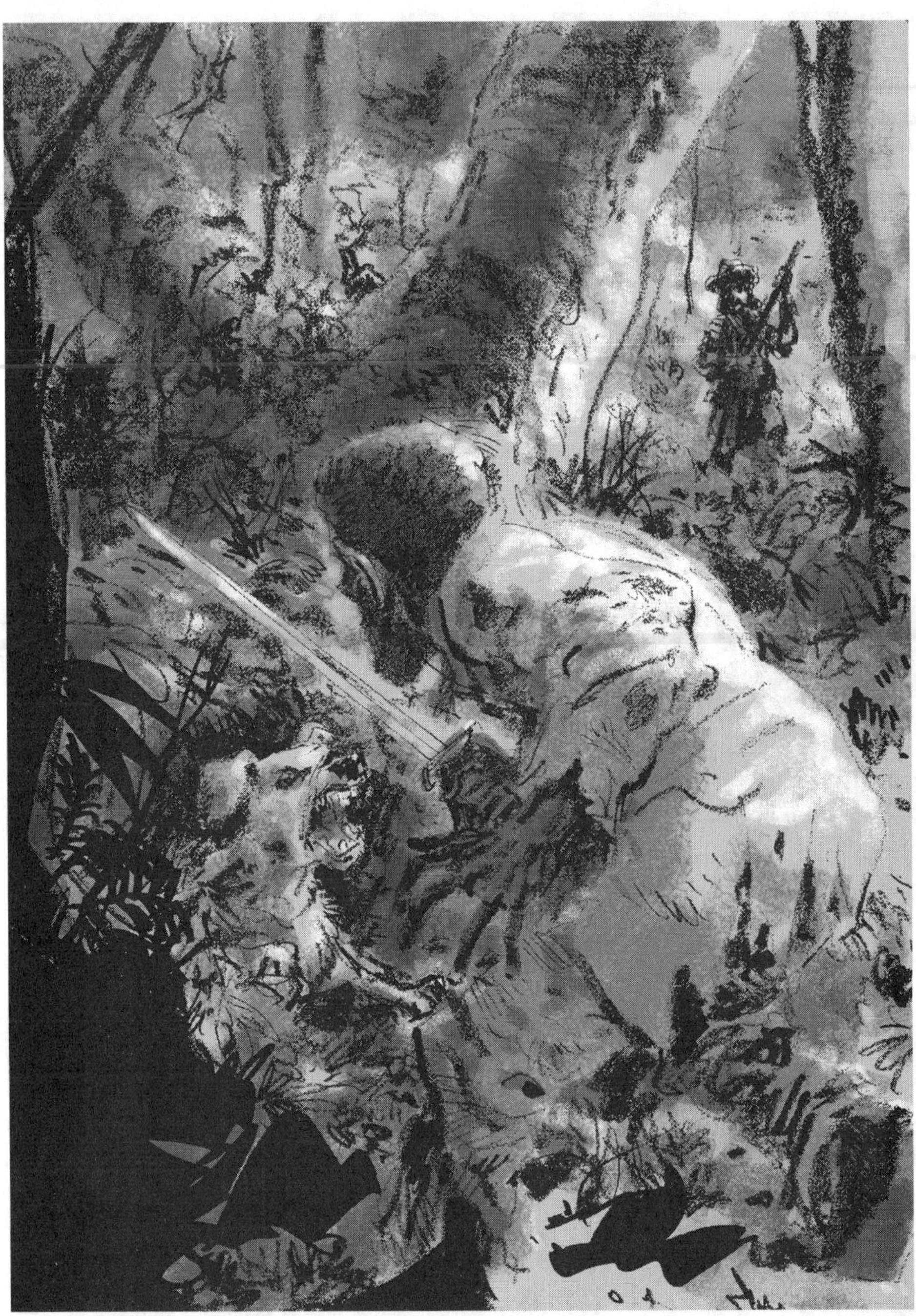

"I KNOW NOT HOW LONG I MIGHT HAVE LED THIS LIFE, IF ACCIDENT HAD NOT BETRAYED ME, A DOG IN THE NEIGHBORHOOD PASSING BY MY HIDING PLACE ONE NIGHT WHILE I WAS OUT, WAS ATTRACTED BY SOME MEAT I HAD IN MY CAVE, AND CRAWLED IN AND STOLE IT, AND WAS COMING OUT JUST AS I RETURNED.

"ON MR. PHIPPS DISCOVERING THE PLACE OF MY CONCEALMENT, HE COCKED HIS GUN AND AIMED AT ME. I REQUESTED HIM NOT TO SHOOT, AND I WOULD GIVE UP, UPON WHICH BE DEMANDED MY SWORD. I DELIVERED IT TO HIM, AND HE BROUGHT ME TO PRISON. DURING THE TIME I WAS PURSUED, I HAD MANY HAIR BREADTH ESCAPES, WHICH YOUR TIME WILL NOT PERMIT YOU TO RELATE. I AM HERE LOADED WITH CHAINS, AND WILLING TO SUFFER THE FATE THAT AWAITS ME."

FROM THE RECORD OF THOMAS R. GRAY:

"*I* SHALL NOT ATTEMPT TO DESCRIBE THE EFFECT OF HIS NARRATIVE, AS TOLD AND COMMENTED ON BY HIMSELF, IN THE CONDEMNED HOLE OF THE PRISON. THE CALM, DELIBERATE COMPOSURE WITH WHICH HE SPOKE OF HIS LATE DEEDS AND INTENTIONS, THE EXPRESSION OF HIS FIEND-LIKE FACE WHEN EXCITED BY ENTHUSIASM, STILL BEARING THE STAINS OF THE BLOOD OF HELPLESS INNOCENCE ABOUT HIM; CLOTHED WITH RAGS AND COVERED WITH CHAINS; YET DARING TO RAISE HIS MANACLED HANDS TO HEAVEN, WITH A SPIRIT SOARING ABOVE THE ATTRIBUTES OF MAN; I LOOKED ON HIM AND MY BLOOD CURDLED IN MY VEINS.

Question. "Do you not find yourself mistaken now?"

Answer. "Was not Christ crucified?"

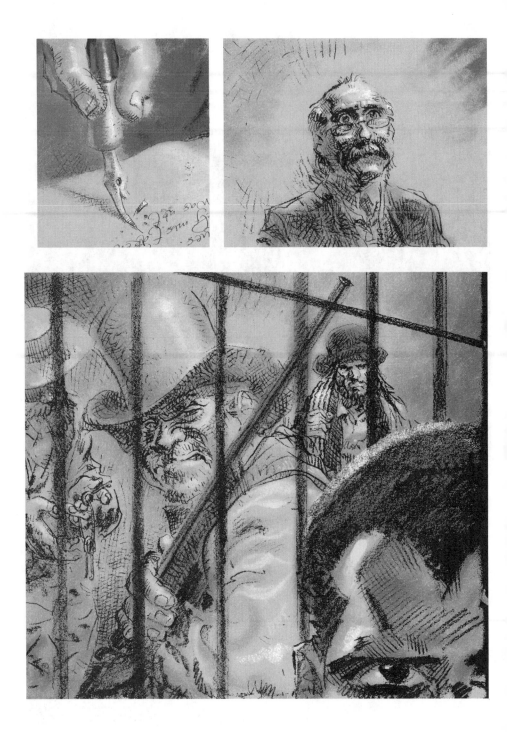

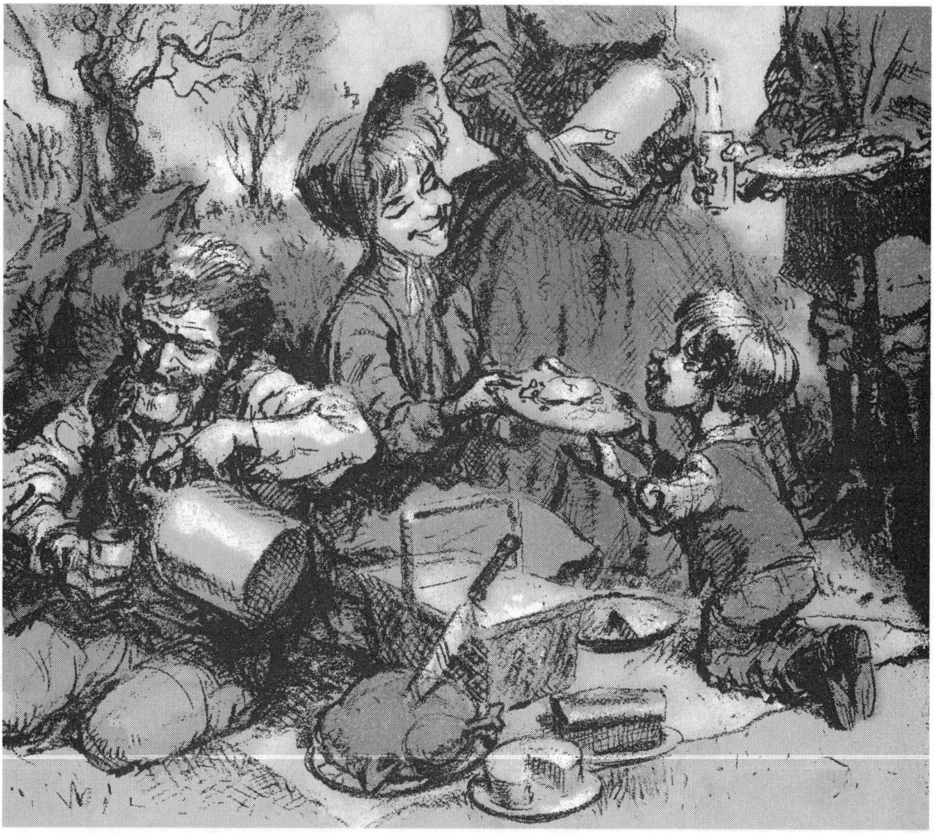

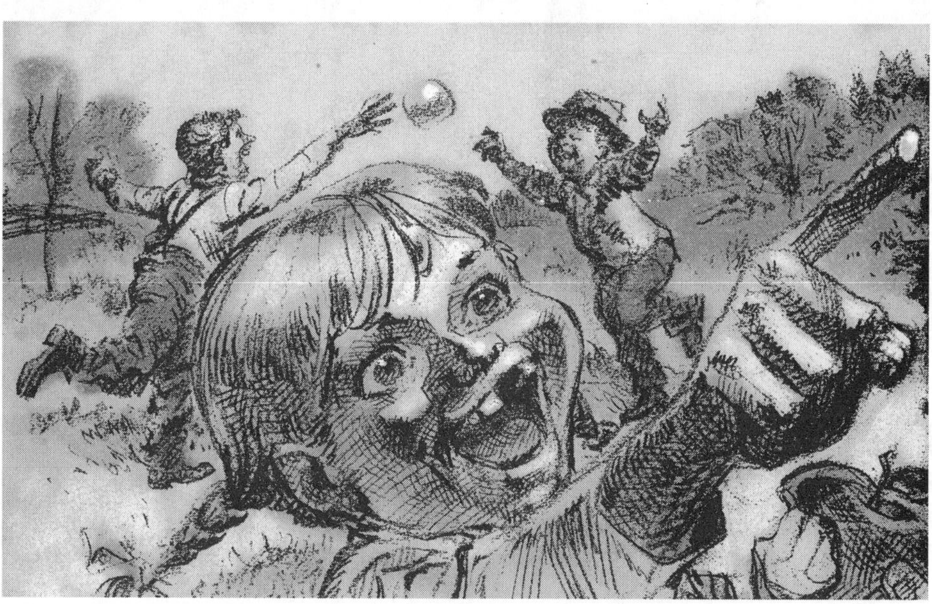

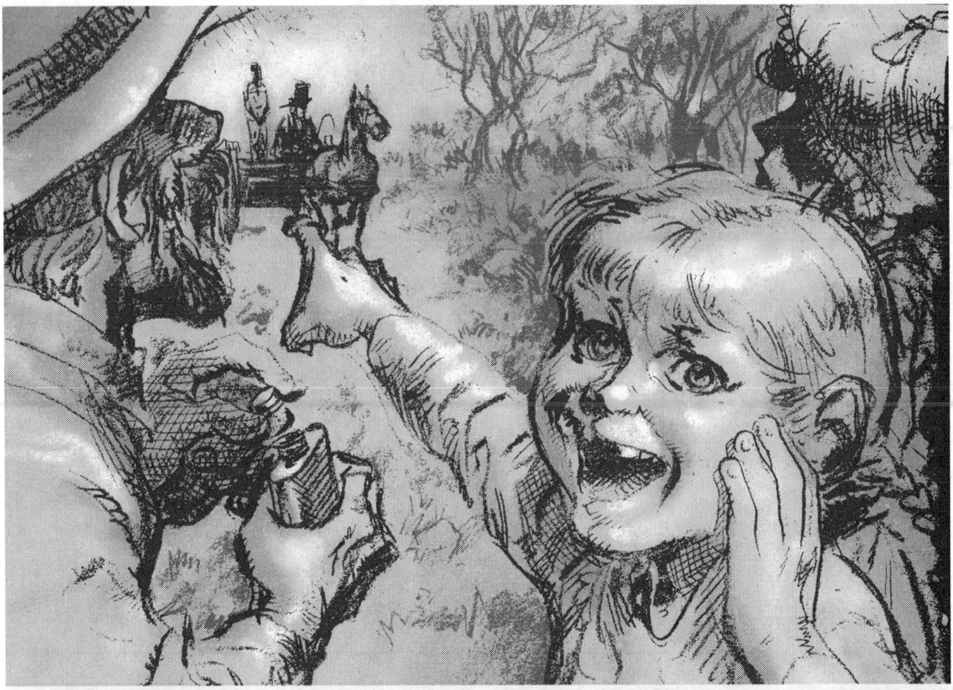

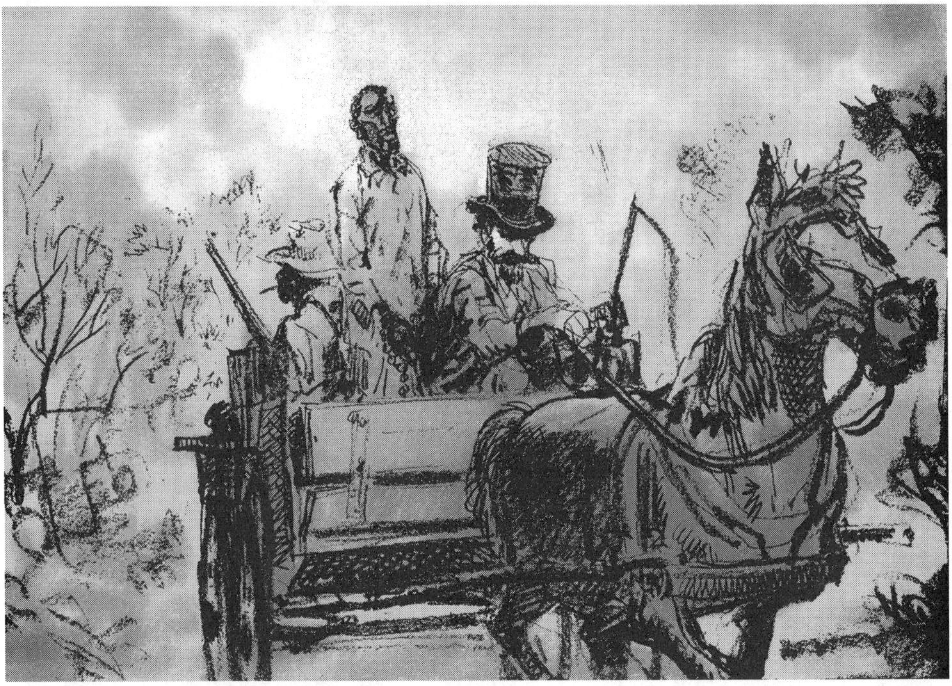

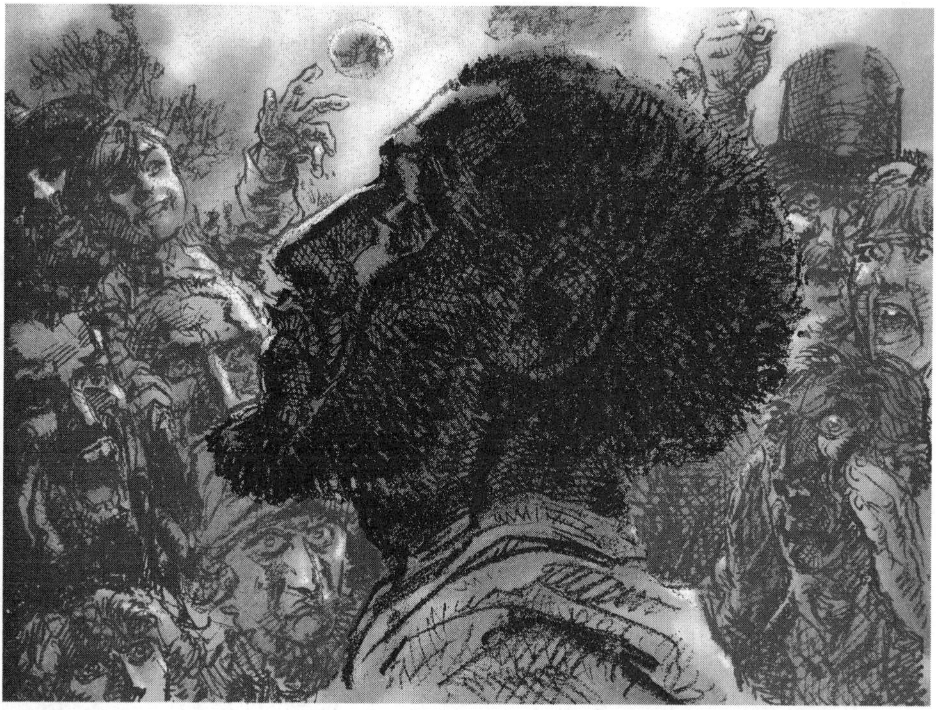

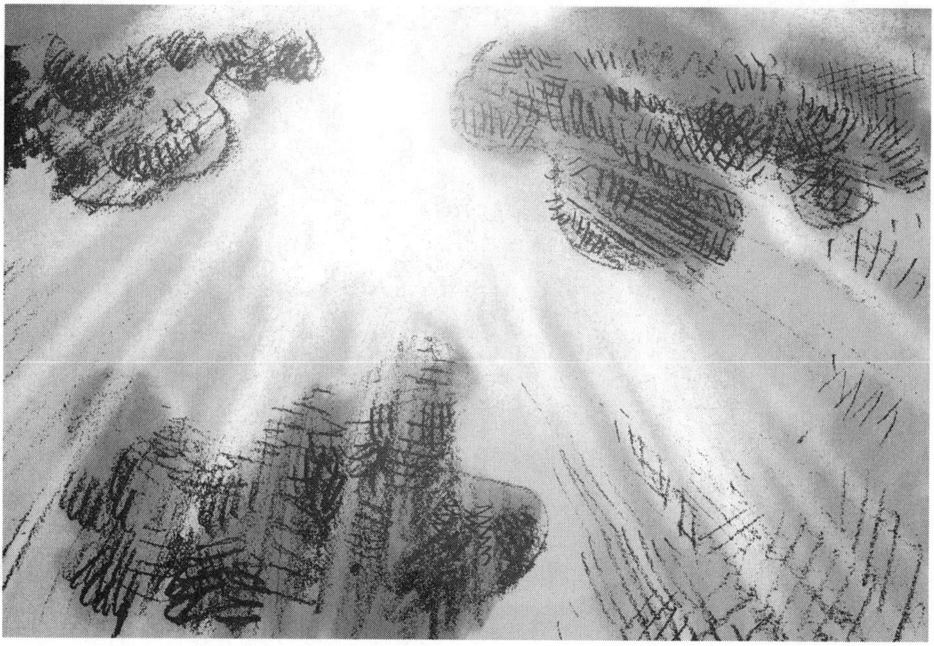

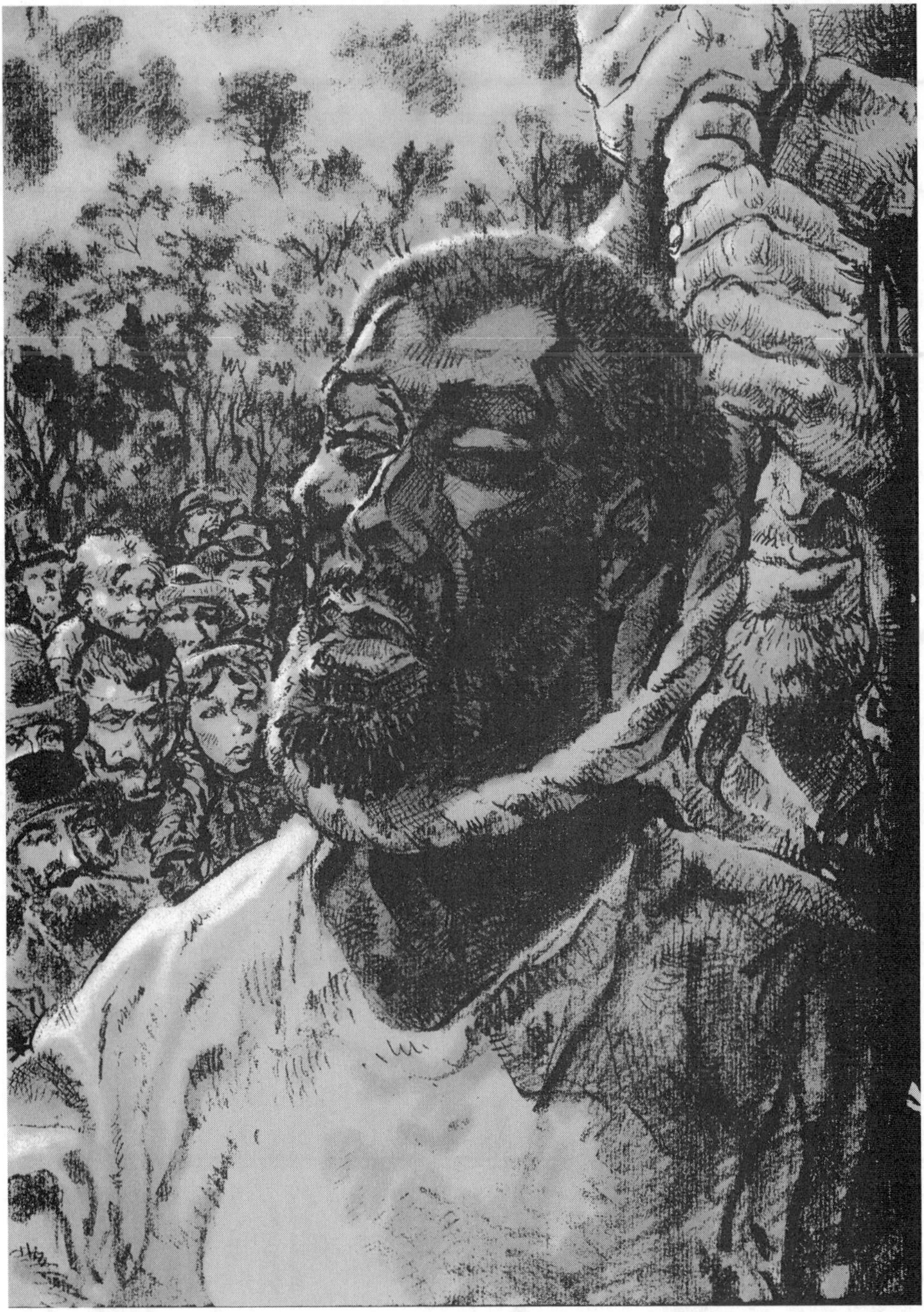

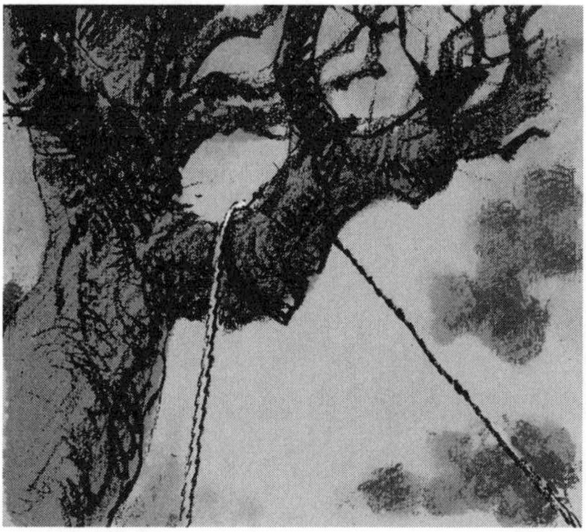

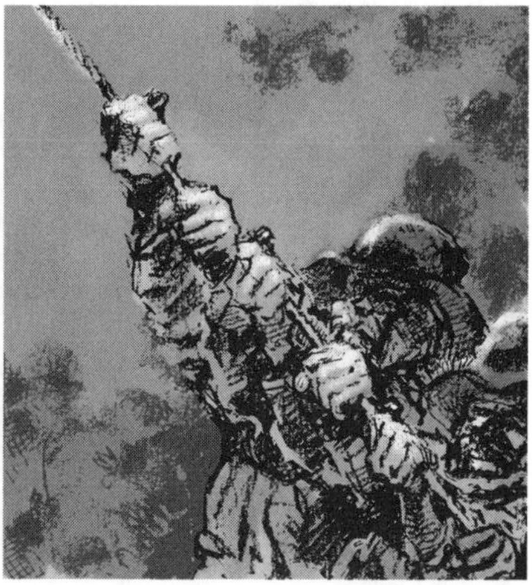

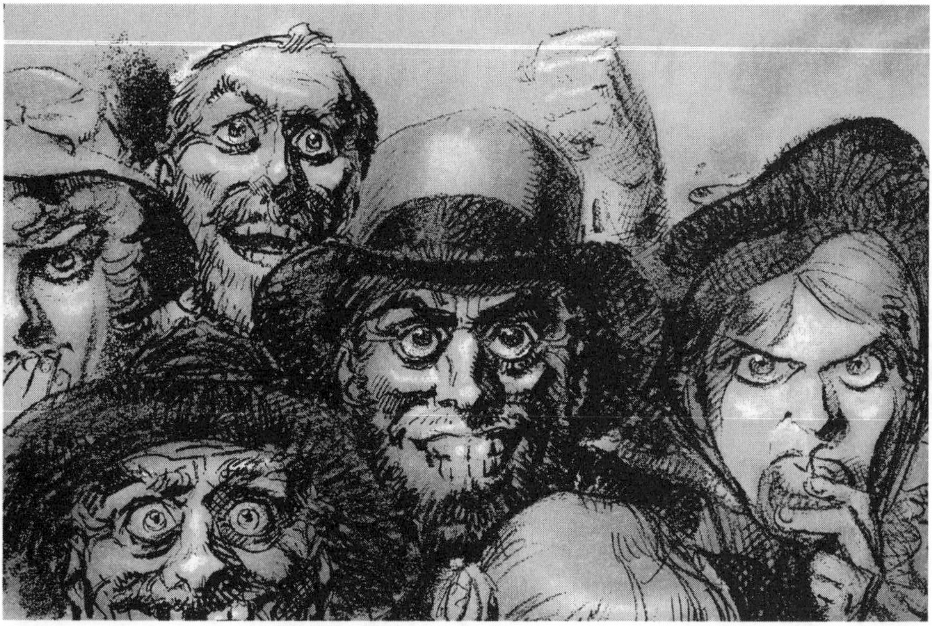

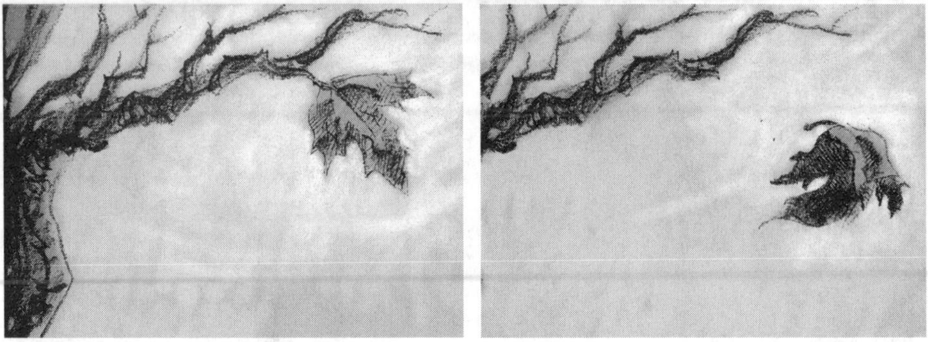

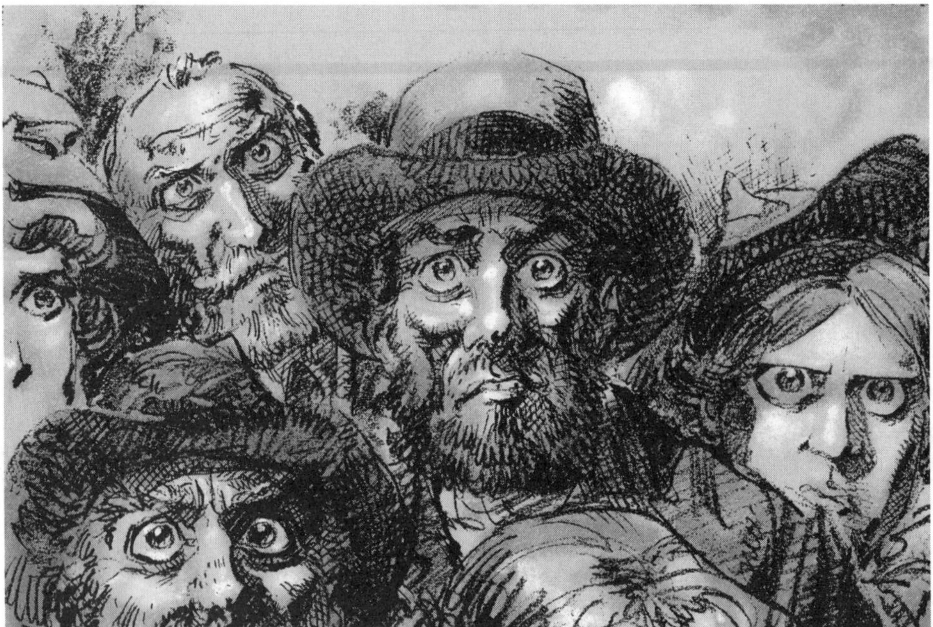

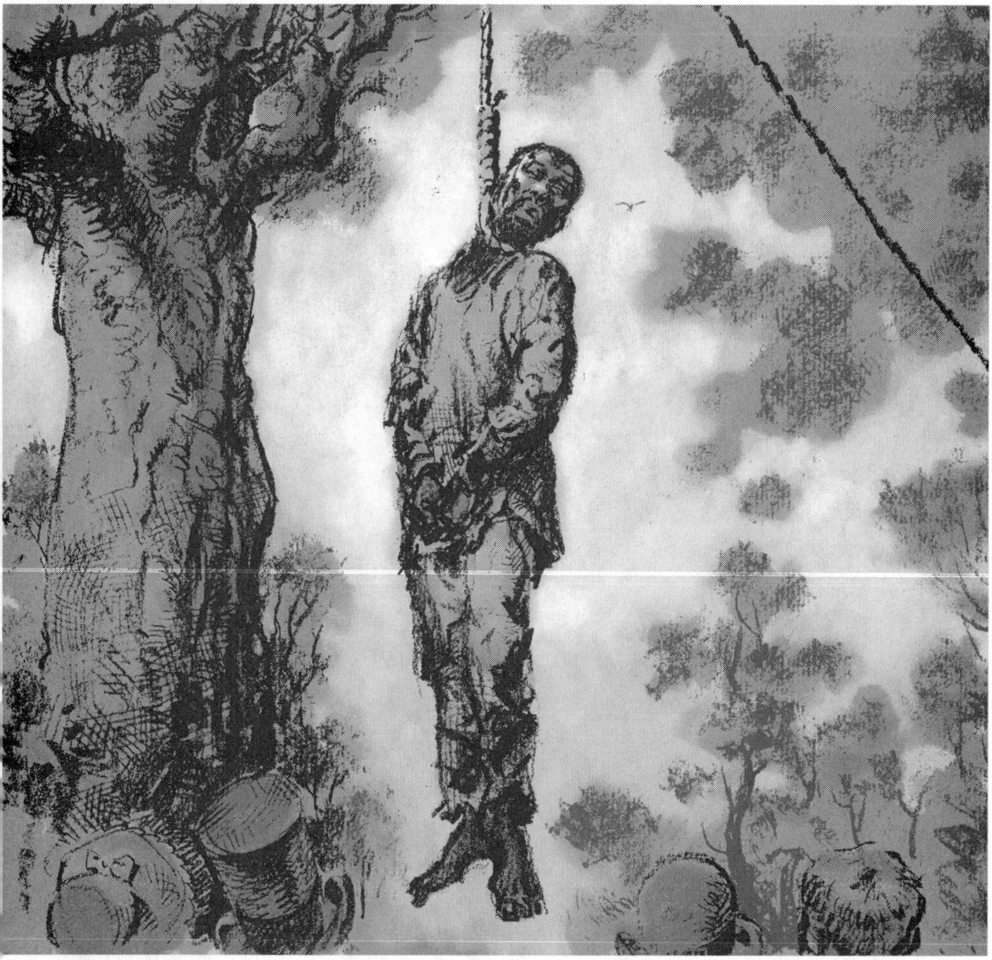

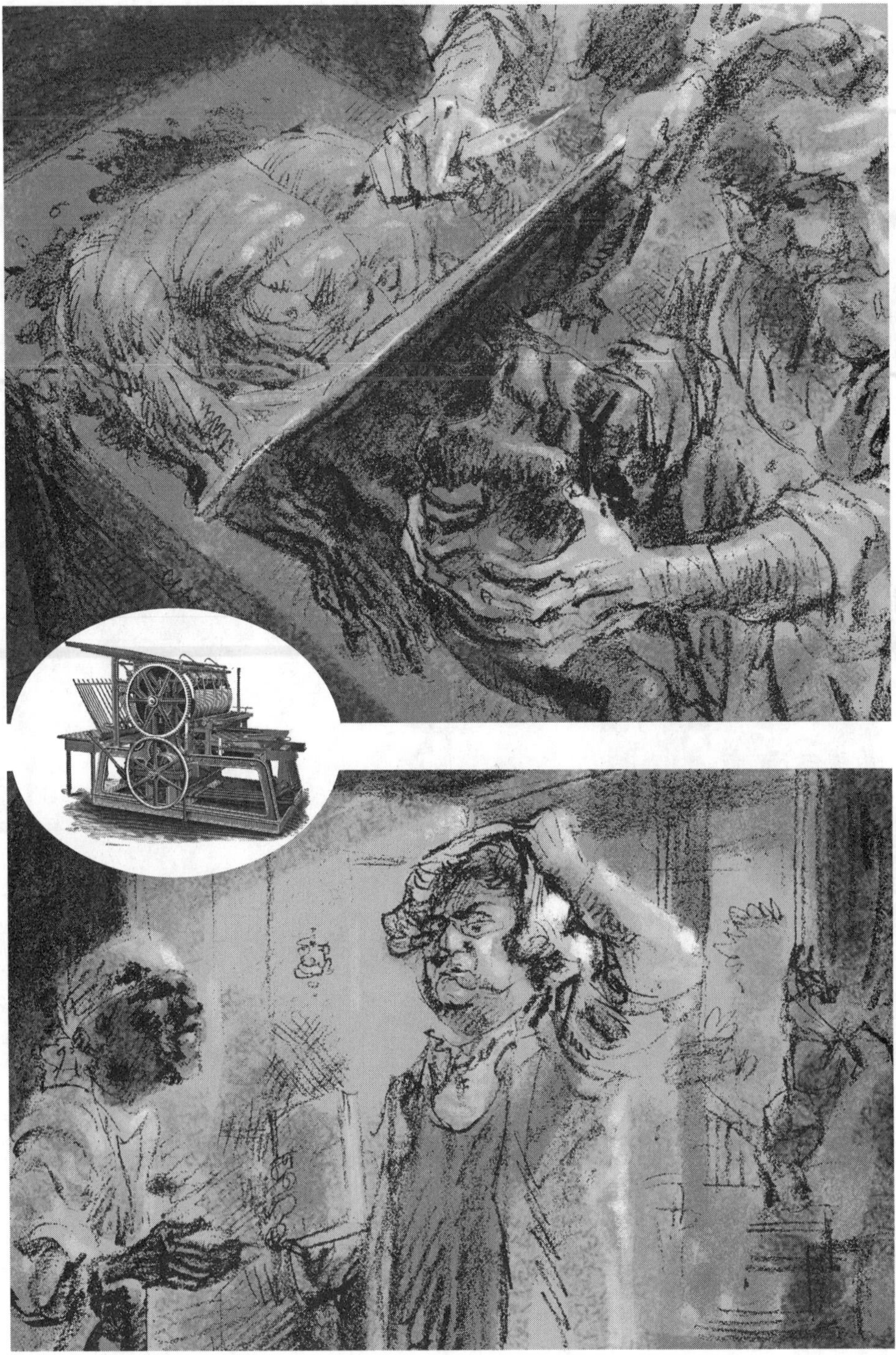

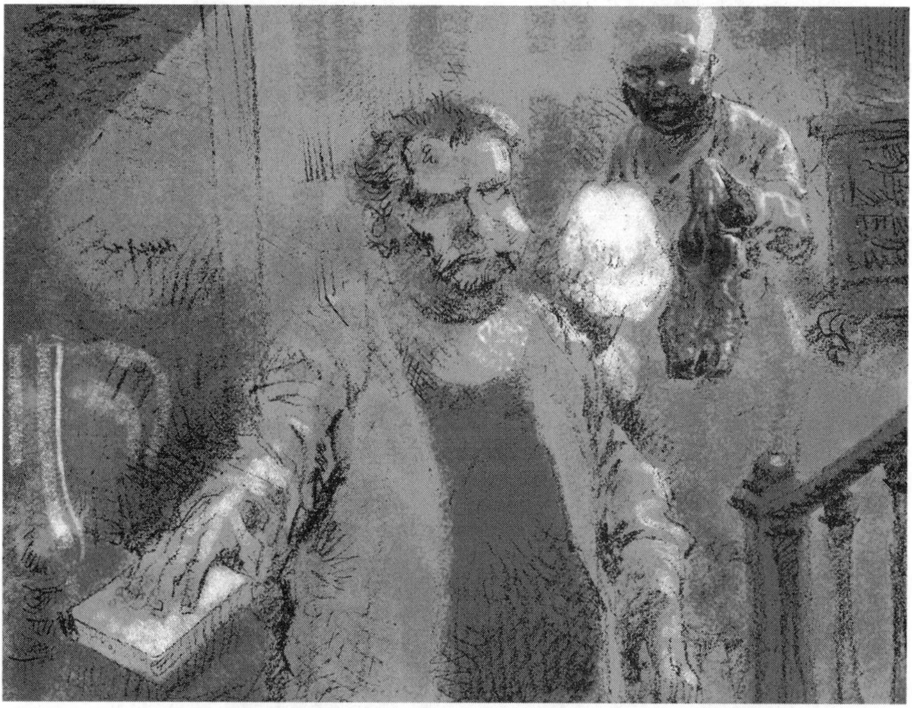

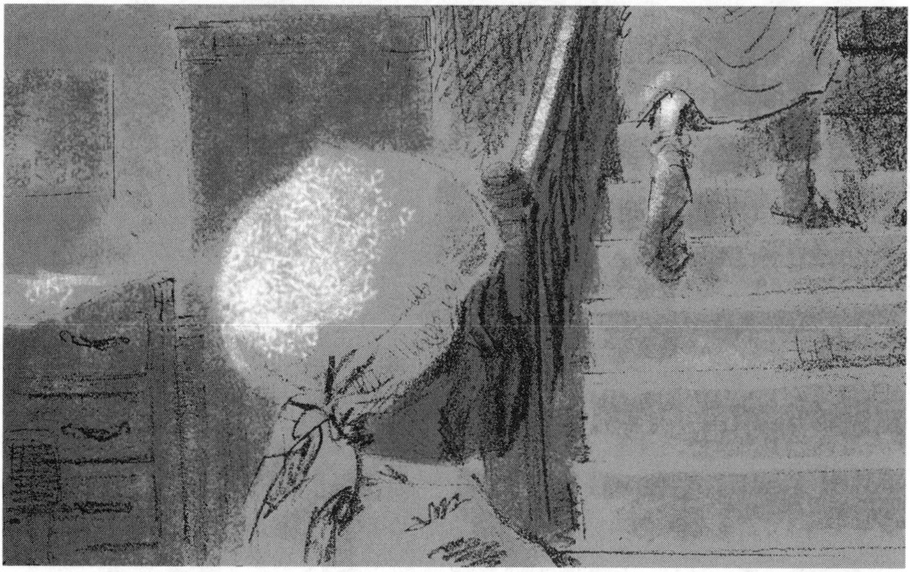

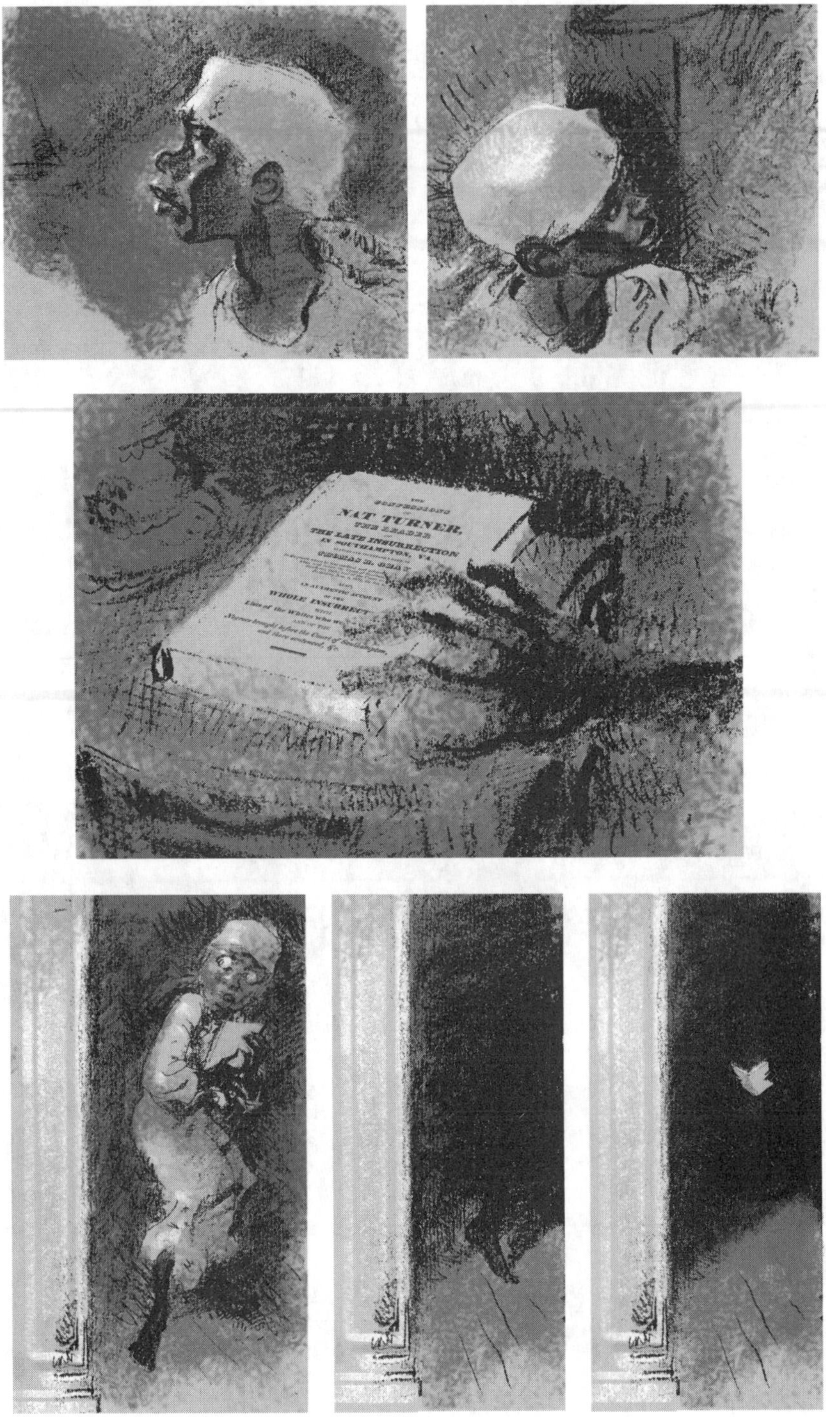
NAT TURNER,
THE LATE INSURRECTION
WHOLE INSURRECT

The
End

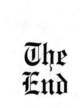

Bibliography

PLOSKI, HARRY A. (EDITOR). REFERENCE LIBRARY OF
BLACK AMERICA. AFRO-AMERICAN PRESS

GRAY, THOMAS. THE CONFESSIONS OF NAT TURNER

OATES, STEPHEN B. THE FIRES OF JUBILEE: NAT
TURNER'S FIERCE. REBELLION HARPER COLLINS

BISSON, TERRY. NAT TURNER: SLAVE REVOLT LEADER.
GROLIER INC.

CANOT, THEODORE. CAPT. ADVENTURES OF AN
AMERICAN SLAVER. DOVER PUBLICATIONS

BOK, FRANCIS ESCAPE FROM SLAVERY.
ST. MARTIN'S PRESS

THOMAS, VELMA MAIA. LEST WE FORGET.
CROWN PUBLISHING GROUP

LIBRARY OF CONGRESS SLAVE NARRATIVE COLLECTION
HTTP://MEMORY.LOC.GOV:8081/AMMEM/SNHTML/SNHOME.HTML

Image Comics, Inc.

ERIK LARSEN - PUBLISHER
TODD MCFARLANE - PRESIDENT
MARC SILVESTRI - CEO
JIM VALENTINO - VICE-PRESIDENT

ERIC STEPHENSON - EXECUTIVE DIRECTOR
MARK HAVEN BRITT - DIRECTOR OF MARKETING
THAO LE - ACCOUNTS MANAGER
TRACI HUI - ADMINISTRATIVE ASSISTANT
JOE KEATINGE - TRAFFIC MANAGER
ALLEN HUI - PRODUCTION MANAGER
JONATHAN CHAN - PRODUCTION ARTIST
DREW GILL - PRODUCTION ARTIST
CHRIS GIARRUSSO - PRODUCTION ARTIST

HTTP://WWW.IMAGECOMICS.COM